SpringerBriefs in Economics

More information about this series at http://www.springer.com/series/8876

Noriatsu Matsui · Yukio Ikemoto
Editors

Solidarity Economy and Social Business

New Models for a New Society

Springer

Editors
Noriatsu Matsui
Faculty of Economics
Teikyo University
Hachioji
Tokyo
Japan

Yukio Ikemoto
Institute for Advanced Studies on Asia
The University of Tokyo
Bunkyo-ku
Tokyo
Japan

ISSN 2191-5504 ISSN 2191-5512 (electronic)
SpringerBriefs in Economics
ISBN 978-4-431-55470-7 ISBN 978-4-431-55471-4 (eBook)
DOI 10.1007/978-4-431-55471-4

Library of Congress Control Number: 2014960136

Springer Tokyo Heidelberg New York Dordrecht London

Printed on acid-free paper

Springer Japan KK is part of Springer Science+Business Media (www.springer.com)

Preface

With an ever-greater disparity between the world's rich and poor, actions have been taken to remove the imperfections and remedy malfunctions of the market mechanism. An underlying theme of these activities is to connect people and make them directly visible to one another; thus the integrating concept of the "solidarity economy" emerges. This book presents theoretical examinations of why and how connecting people yields different results from those of the market mechanism alone. Adam Smith emphasized the importance of "sympathy" among people and the role of the "impartial spectator" in order to control otherwise reckless markets. These major concepts form the basis of the solidarity economy.

It already has been a while since the discussion on social business became widespread and intense in the world. Many ideas to make a better world were put into practice in the form of social business. However, the significance and meanings of social business have not been understood properly yet. It is our belief that the various forms of social business would play important roles for the new society since it would be a way to connect people more directly than before. It is expected to make the business of solving the problems of society in such a way as to achieve sustainability and expanding operations at the same time.

The purpose of this book is to discuss the characteristics and significance of social business. Social business can be utilized to achieve various targets for human development not only in developing countries but also in industrialized countries. It is being increasingly recognized that social business is an effective form toward solving social problems in the world in which neither government nor private sector can find truly effective solutions for those problems.

The first chapter discusses the background and necessity of social business by arguing the deficiency of the traditional model of the market in the twenty-first-century world. Chapter 1 shows that our interest in a solidarity economy is based on research on Amartya Sen's capability approach and Grameen Bank's micro-credit. The discussions on information and reasoning are elaborated.

Chapter 2 examines Grameen Bank of Bangladesh as a pioneer of microcredit for the poor in the developing world. Characteristics of Grameen Bank operation and major factors of success of microcredit are discussed. Recent movements in microfinance and inclusive finance to provide a variety of financial access and services to the poor in the world are briefly surveyed. Offering microcredit to borrowers in poor communities not only in developing countries but also in the EU and North America is expanding. Chapter 3 introduces microcredit pilot project activities in Spain as a Grameen model operation.

Chapter 4 gives an overview of a Grameen social business to provide solar power energy, biogas generation, and an improved cooking stove, Grameen Shakti. In a country like Bangladesh, the growing need for stable and higher energy is becoming acute. Chapters 5 and 6 discuss provision of nutritious food, yogurt, and clean water to rural people. These activities are intended to create income-generating opportunities for local poor people on top of improving nutritious food and water quality.

Chapter 7 discusses the role of the local currency movement for the purpose of regional revitalization of local business and community development. The chapter discusses an experiment in exchange transaction through a local currency in Yamaguchi, Japan. Chapter 8 examines activities related to organic agriculture in Japan, Korea, and Thailand. In all cases solidarity between producers and consumers plays an important role. Certification in Fair Trade of coffee is a mechanism to help move toward solving environmental concerns and alleviating poverty. The case of coffee in Vietnam is discussed in Chap. 9. Chapter 10 introduces the development of social business backed by the government of Korea through legislation. This final chapter includes some local case studies from Korea.

This volume is written to be suitable for practitioners, scholars, and graduate and advanced undergraduate students by virtue of its valuable resources as well as its references to prepare for practical activities. It is expected that this book will be helpful for those people in designing and promoting further ways to connect people, thus to enhance solidarity, in the new and better society to come. Keywords, a brief summary, and topics for further consideration are provided for each chapter.

Our project has been supported by a Grant-in-Aid for Scientific Research from the Japan Society for the Promotion of Sciences (Project number: 25380327, project title: Utilization of Social Business for Human Development: Comparison between Bangladesh and Spain, project term: 2013–2015). We would like to acknowledge with deep gratitude the financial assistance received from Akita University, Teikyo University, and The University of Tokyo. We also greatly appreciate the valuable comments and collaboration that we have received from Dr. Masamitsu Kurata of JICA.

Hachioji, Tokyo Noriatsu Matsui
Bunkyo-ku, Tokyo Yukio Ikemoto

Contents

Chapter 1
Solidarity and Social Business: Theoretical Background

Yukio Ikemoto and Noriatsu Matsui

Abstract If the problems that we are facing today are often caused by the failure of the market mechanism, in which individuals are separated from each other, the problems may be solved by reconnecting people, which means solidarity among people, whether they call it solidarity or not. There are many types of activities for this purpose from local groups such as microcredit in developing countries to fair trade at the global level. The ways to connect people can be classified into two: One is the face-to-face relationship and the other is the labels that convey the information of the other party. In either case, the information takes important roles to achieve better conditions. This point was emphasized by Amartya Sen in his book (The Idea of Justice. Harvard University Press, Cambridge, 2009). Solidarity has an intrinsic value for human life because it will improve our health and happiness. But it has a more important role for justice. As Sen argued, we need more information about our life in order to make our life better. The capability approach is a way to widen our informational base to various aspects of our life. Another point is that we do not assume human beings are selfish. We are human beings who care for other people suffering from poverty. However, we cannot neglect the market mechanism. In order to make the solidarity economy sustainable, we need business methods. And the social business is one of the solutions, various types of which are shown in this book.

Keywords Solidarity · Capability approach · Information · Reasoning · Poverty and inequality · Altruism · Sustainability

---

Y. Ikemoto
Institute for Advanced Studies on Asia, The University of Tokyo, 7-3-1 Hongo, Bunkyo-ku, Tokyo 113-0033, Japan
e-mail: ikemoto@ioc.u-tokyo.ac.jp

N. Matsui (✉)
Teikyo University, 359 Otsuka, Hachioji, Tokyo 192-0395, Japan
e-mail: noripmat@main.teikyo-u.ac.jp

N. Matsui and Y. Ikemoto (eds.), *Solidarity Economy and Social Business*, SpringerBriefs in Economics, DOI 10.1007/978-4-431-55471-4_1

1.1 Introduction

Globalization is bringing about big changes in our lives today. While the Internet is connecting people around the world, globalization of the economy has increased the gap between the rich and the poor in various ways. The rich are becoming richer while the poor are becoming poorer. If globalization of the economy is pursuing the market mechanism at the global level and the increasing gap is being caused by the failure of the market mechanism, we may overcome the problems by reconnecting people who have been separated from each other by the market mechanism. The kinds of activities that try to challenge and overcome those problems can be found in various aspects of our lives. They take very different forms, but they can be categorized as "solidarity economy" in the sense that people may be united to solve problems without leaving them separated and desperate in the face of the fierce forces of the market mechanism.

The concept of solidarity economy has been drawing attention especially in the 2000s. In 2001 the World Social Forum (WSF) was held in Porto Alegre, Brazil. In 2007 the Asian Solidarity Economy Forum (ASEF) was held in Manila, The Philippines. Activities based on solidarity, even though they may not refer to solidarity, have been increasing. In Japan, after the East Japan Earthquake of March 11, 2011, the Japanese word "*kizuna*," which means "solidarity (bonds/ties)," became very popular among Japanese people and many of them joined the activities of volunteer organizations and NGOs to help those who suffered from the earthquake and tsunami. Those who lost assets because of the earthquake and tsunami lost entitlement in the sense described by Amartya Sen and cannot survive in the market mechanism. When people find others suffering, they tend to help them, which is a part of human nature that has evolved throughout the long history of mankind.

This is true not only in a country or in a community but also between the people in developed countries and the people in developing countries. Even within developing countries we can find solidarity. Microcredit of Grameen Bank in Bangladesh, which will be explained in detail in this book, is based on small groups of women who help each other to repay their debts. Microeconomics, which is based on the assumption that human beings are selfish, may understand that these kinds of small groups of women keep watch over other people to pressure them to repay debt. But this view fails to see the aspect of mutual help. Not just to be watched but the help of others human beings can achieve much more by utilizing their ability more fully. In this sense microeconomics, which assumes selfish human beings, underestimates human ability. One way to overcome the problems that may be caused by the traditional economic thinking is to understand that human beings are not only selfish but also altruistic at the same time, a concept that can be used to attempt to approach a more equitable society.

From an historical point of view, we may be at a stage of transition from marketism towards solidarity. In the past, the Industrial Revolution and citizens' revolutions liberated people from the restrictions of the old regime and enabled them to move towards a market economy. In the eighteenth century, Adam Smith had to defend the market economy because the restrictions of society in those days limited the free economic activities of individuals and was an obstacle to the Industrial Revolution. However, at the end of the twentieth century, in the 1990s, the market economy reached a peak and at the same time its problems, which were caused by excessive individualism and marketism, became apparent. Now in such a situation, we may be at another historical turning point and approaching an age of solidarity.

Because the amount of information that can be conveyed in the market mechanism is so limited, we cannot achieve a desirable society solely through the use of the market mechanism. Dealing with environmental problems is an example. One cause of environmental problems is that the market does not sufficiently convey information about environmental problems, with the end result that consumers do not pay enough money to cover the costs for the prevention of environmental destruction. For example, consumers of coffee in developed countries usually are not aware of the fact that coffee grown in developing countries often causes some destruction of the environment. Consumers may be responsible for the environmental destruction by demanding cheap coffee, which may worsen the lives of coffee farmers who then cannot afford to pay enough attention to environmental protection and with the end result that the environment is destroyed.

If the problems are caused by limited information, a way to solve the problems is to increase the amount of information. If consumers of coffee are to understand the fact that the coffee they consume is grown at the cost of impoverishing coffee farmers and destroying the environment, consumers may not choose inexpensive coffee even if the prices are lower. What the Fair Trade and other certified coffee organizations are doing is to convey, by certification or labels, the reality of the plight of coffee farmers and the negative impact on the environment, which has led consumers to make more ethical choices in which coffee they buy. This system of labels and certificates promotes a more positive role to connect farmers and consumers and nurtures a type of solidarity economy.

A large variety of activities can be included in the category of solidarity economy, but they have a common feature in that they try to solve the problems that are caused by the market mechanism by attempting to connect people in various forms. The problems include what the market mechanism cannot solve or what the market mechanism itself causes such as poverty and environmental destruction. A solidarity economy not only may share the means by which people are connected; it also includes different groups of people, from the radicals who try to replace the market completely by solidarity to the more moderate ones who try to maintain the market mechanism while complementing it with solidarity. However, since the collapse of the socialist countries in the 1990s, the moderate way has become more realistic and so the solidarity economy should be able to survive alongside the market economy. Therefore what will be explored in this book are the activities that try to solve the problems of poverty and environment in the framework of the market economy. The scope of activities varies from the face-to-face relationships composed of several people to global relationships such as Fair Trade which connect consumers in developed countries and farmers in developing countries.

Our interest in solidarity economy started from research on Amartya Sen's capability approach and Grameen Bank's microcredit. Amartya Sen's capability approach is a concept to capture human well-being by what the person can do and can be, not by income. Income is just a means to do something, and if we take into consideration the diversity of human beings, what a person can achieve may be different from what others can achieve even though their income level may be the same. For example, if a person is handicapped or socially discriminated against, she or he cannot achieve the same level of well-being as other people with the same level of income. Sen's approach is thus very different from mainstream economics which excludes non-economic information.

Another important point of Sen's capability approach is that it does not exclude altruistic motivation. Economics assumes that human beings are selfish and try to maximize only their own interests. On the other hand, solidarity economy includes many kinds of activities that pursue the interests of others, sometimes at the cost of self-interest. This is what Sen calls "agency". The activities of the women's group of Grameen Bank that we observed in Bangladesh include this sense of solidarity. Thus, it is understood that it is inappropriate to explain their activities only in terms of economics. It is very unfair and disgraceful for them to explain altruistic activities in terms of selfish motivations alone. Therefore we need an approach that does not exclude altruistic motivation. We know very well that we can achieve much more with the help of others than what we can do alone. Since we started our research based on the capability approach, we have found many activities that are based on broader information and close relationships. For example, organic farming needs face-to-face relationships to convey more information and to allow people to help each other. In this book we try to show these activities in the framework of solidarity economy. Our approach is very different from that of the traditional solidarity economy. It may be said that we present a theoretical framework for solidarity economy, which can include a large variety of activities.

In the next section, we will discuss the intrinsic value of solidarity from the point of view of health and happiness before discussing the economic aspects of solidarity. In Sect. 1.2, by making comparisons with mainstream economics, it will be shown that Amartya Sen's capability approach has an affinity with solidarity economy in the sense that both of them pursue better situations by broadening the informational base and emphasizing consideration of other people's needs. In Sect. 1.3 the capability approach is explained in terms of two points: (1) capability and (2) reasoning, as the basis for the discussion in this book.

1.2 Health and Happiness: Intrinsic Value of Solidarity

In economics, it is assumed that human beings are basically interested only in their own utility and that the utility is usually determined only by the quantities of the goods and services consumed by individuals. There is no room for consideration of other people. If a person helps other people, it is because it will increase his or her own utility irrespective of the utility of the others. However, the others may suffer from poverty, so they may not help people unless it increases their own utility directly or indirectly. This is very different from altruism in its true sense. On the contrary, a person's altruistic conduct in the true sense, which may not increase his or her own utility, would be considered "irrational" in terms of economics. In economics, all conduct is explained as selfish.

In the past, the classical utilitarian insisted that we should choose a society that maximizes the sum of the utilities of all members of the society. It was very democratic in the sense that it reflected the utility of the majority of the society, and it was useful during the era of citizens' revolutions. They could insist on a more egalitarian society if it could increase the sum of utility by raising the utility of the poor majority. Adding up the utilities of people means that the individual utilities are comparable with each other. In other words, my utility is comparable with yours. In this sense people can understand how other people feel, which is the basis of solidarity economy. However, the modern utilitarian and also traditional economics rejected the idea of adding the utilities of people by accepting the criticism of Robbins (1932). He insisted that a person's utility cannot be compared with that of others. This was a serious problem because now we cannot compare the utility of ten dollars between rich and poor people, even though ten dollars is insignificant for the rich while it has a vital importance for the poor. Even in this situation we cannot say that the income transfer of ten dollars is socially desirable. This clearly shows that human beings in economics are isolated and it stops thinking about redistribution problems in order to make society better. Instead it concentrates on showing the efficiency of the market mechanism in which isolated individuals behave selfishly. If we pursue a better society, we need to overcome the limitation of the market economy, and the solidarity economy is a way worthy of exploration.

After Lionel Robbins' criticism, economics abandoned the comparison of utilities between people. However, human beings have an ability to understand how other people feel. Adam Smith emphasized sympathy in his book *The Theory of Moral Sentiments* (1759) and discussed how to achieve a better society by sympathy and by being an "impartial observer." While often regarded as the advocate of capitalism, Smith's *Wealth of Nations* (1776) is harshly critical of the shortcomings of unrestrained free enterprise and monopoly. It is interesting to think how the sympathy of human beings evolved in human history. Richard Wilkinson insisted in his book *The Impact of Inequality* (2009) that the human body evolved throughout its long history towards living in an equal society such that human health would be damaged if humans were to live in an unequal society. According to him, the reason for the deteriorating health is the intolerance of the human body to an unequal society. In the hunting and gathering society, which accounts for almost all of the several million years of human history, there existed a very equal society, and so the human body evolved to live in an equal society. Perhaps people who help each other could survive longer and weak people could survive with the help of the others in the community. In the community it was advantageous to express one's feeling to others, and the human face evolved to express many more kinds of feelings than those of other animals. Those people whose faces expressed their needs may have been helped while those whose faces did not express them were not helped and could not survive. On the other hand, human beings developed the ability to understand how other people feel and to help others when they are in need; in other words they developed sympathy.

Thus human evolution has reflected the efforts of human beings to solve the problems that they faced by solidarity. In the past 30 years since the 1980s, socio-epidemiological research has been devoted to proving the impact of an unequal society on human health and now this view is widely accepted. It was in the 1980s when society became more and more unequal in the UK and the USA under so-called Thatcherism and Reaganomics, respectively. A direct reason why we are seeking solidarity is because it is good for our health and because we can live happily, whereas our health will be damaged in an individually isolated and severely competitive society.

1.3 The Capability Approach for Better Society

Besides the direct effect of solidarity on human health as mentioned in the previous section, solidarity has an indirect role in overcoming the deficiency of the market mechanism.

Adam Smith, who is known as the father of economics, is often considered an adherent of the market mechanism, but he did not think that the market mechanism could solve every problem. Rather, Smith, as a moral philosopher, had an idea to control it by his concept of "impartial observer." If the market mechanism guides us to a socially undesirable situation, he considered that it should be checked from the point of view of an impartial observer. This two-facedness of Smith, that is, being an adherent of marketism and being a moral philosopher, is still useful today, and a fair society should be founded on the balance of these two characteristics. Contrary to Adam Smith, unfortunately the present age has lost the balance and marketism has been pursued excessively. We can observe harmful impacts such as poverty and environmental problems, which cannot be solved effectively by the market mechanism. We need ethical considerations in this aspect, and Adam Smith considered it from the point of view of the relationship with others. Even for Smith, individuals are not isolated.

This aspect of Smith is emphasized in Amartya Sen's *The Idea of Justice* (2009). Sen has been inquiring into what are the conditions of a "good society," which became unpopular among economists after Kenneth J. Arrow proved the impossibility theorem in 1951. Sen showed that the problem is caused by the very limited information about economics and insisted that we need to enrich our informational base to overcome this problem and to discuss what is better from the point of view of our society. And for this purpose he proposed the capability approach, which focuses on what people can do and can be as the informational base, rather than utility, income, or resources. Sen discusses in his book how to use the concept of capability as the informational base to achieve a better and fairer society, which is closely related to the discussions in this book in two points: (1) capability and (2) reasoning. The concept of capability was created by Sen to capture the human well-being through what people "can do and can be" with the aim of broadening our informational base beyond limited market information. And reasoning broadens our motivation to include altruistic behavior, which is necessary for solidarity. We need not be as selfish as is assumed in economics anymore. These points will be explained in turn in this book.

1.3.1 Amartya Sen's Capability Approach

Amartya Sen's argument started from Arrow's impossibility theorem, which insists that there exists no so-called social welfare function that evaluates the goodness of various social states. This theorem was a fatal blow to economics because it means economics lost ground in judging which economic situation is desirable. Since then, economics gave up thinking about what kind of society is good for us and just concentrated on proving the superiority of the market mechanism. The limitation of this approach is that we cannot go beyond the Pareto optimum. Even though economics stopped thinking about changing our society for the better, some economists still tried to find solutions to overcome the impossibility theorem and Sen was one of them.

In his analysis, the real problem is caused by the poor contents of the information that cannot compare utilities between people and he tried to answer this question by enriching the information about judging the goodness of society. He insisted that human well-being cannot be measured appropriately by utility or income, but by what people can do and can be. What people can do and can be is not just what people are doing or being but what he or she can actually choose. In this sense, it is the extent of choice, or in other words, freedom, which includes not only political freedom but also economic and other freedoms. If we understand human well-being in terms of freedom, development is also measured by freedom.[1] Therefore poverty is a situation that does not achieve the minimum level of human freedom, which may correspond to the basic human needs (BHN) .[2] When we define our informational base in this way, we cannot rely on the market, which excludes a lot of information that we need. Our evaluation has to go beyond the market.

We need more information beyond the market. There are many ways to obtain this information, and solidarity is an important way to do so. By meeting each other, we can exchange a lot of information. With the Fair Trade label, we exchange important information about what the consumers need. By using local currency for exchanging goods and services directly, people get

[1] The title of Sen (1999) denotes this relationship.

[2] The difference between the basic human needs (BHN) approach and the capability approach is that the former focuses on goods and services while the latter focuses on the functionings.

more information about the goods and services traded and produced locally, and thus about local people. In this way, the capability approach is closely related to solidarity economy.

1.3.2 Reasoning: Beyond Selfish Economic Man

In economics it is assumed that each person maximizes solely his or her own utility. This assumption was very useful to make the economic theory simple and easy to understand. However, it lost something important in our lives. On the other hand, the capability approach abandons this assumption. Even though the capability approach chooses the capability as the focal variable, it does not insist on maximizing an index of capability. Since capability is expressed as a set of functionings, we need an index of capability if we want to maximize it. But it is very difficult, or almost impossible, for all people to agree on only one index reflecting human diversity. In this situation we have to rely on reasoned public discussion. Thus reasoning takes an important role in the capability approach. There is no simple formula or theory that answers the solution for us if we input data of capability in the formula. What we need is just a comparison between alternatives that are available to us. We do not need a theory that gives us the best solution if we cannot achieve it. A more realistic problem is to choose from achievable alternatives.[3] For example, if our problem is to choose between a situation in which people lack basic capabilities such as health and education and a situation in which people satisfy those capabilities, we would easily agree which we should choose.

On the other hand, we may have a very different evaluation of more specific functionings such as playing basketball, and it is not easy to agree on whether we should take some action for everybody to have such functionings. People are very diversified in this world, which makes it very difficult to agree on public action. However, theory or approach should take such diversity into consideration. It is rather dangerous to seek theory by ignoring such diversity.[4] We have to accept the diversity of the reality rather than neglect it.

Sen insists on using capability as our informational base, but he did not insist on maximizing it. A person may prefer to contribute to social objectives such as poverty eradication instead of maximizing his or her own utility. He or she may sacrifice his or her own well-being to help poor people. Because people can reason out what to do, we should not exclude altruistic motives. (This does not mean that Sen insists on being altruistic in every aspect of our life. He said we should allow for altruistic motives.) Sometimes a person may help other people for his or her

---

[3] This approach is called the comparative approach while the other, which aims to find the best solution, is called the transcendental approach.

[4] Sen explains this through the analogy of a stopped watch which can show the correct time exactly twice a day. We need a watch that may not be exact but can show approximate time useful for our daily life.

own satisfaction. In this case the behavior is not altruistic but self-interested. Sen distinguished these two cases by defining the altruistic behaviors in the true sense as those which do not increase his or her own utility and called it "agency".

1.4 Sustainability of Solidarity Economy

We have explained the difference between economic theory and solidarity economy from the informational base and motivations. Whereas economic theory tries to explain everything based on self-interest, we can explain non-selfish behavior as it is, which is not only more realistic but also not insulting those people who are really altruistic. For example, in the case of Grameen Bank, women form groups of five persons. Economic theory explains its role as watching each other to repay the debt. On the other hand, solidarity economy will explain it as mutual help to repay it, which is more realistic and more in line with what we observed in Bangladesh. It is insulting to the people whose motive is really altruistic to explain their behavior as selfish.

They are pursuing different objectives and it is not easy to compare them by a single indicator such as income. If a main objective of solidarity economy is poverty alleviation, it must achieve better results than the market economy in this respect. In economic aspects, we have to ask whether it is sustainable in the market economy because we are living in the market economy and it is impossible to eliminate market forces. As for the case of fair trade, it can be sustainable so long as the consumers are willing to pay higher (and fairer) prices for the products and the farmers are producing good products which are competitive enough with the products in the marketplace.

In some cases solidarity can be more productive than isolated individualism. Higher productivity through solidarity can be explained by using game theory. A greater gain from cooperation may be obtained in some settings in game theory, but game theory essentially assumes selfish individual players. Solidarity economy includes and respects the altruistic aspect of human characteristics with and beyond the selfish individualistic aspect, which is a critical difference between solidarity and game theory.

1.5 Social Business in Solidarity Economy

In this section it is argued that social business is an expression of solidarity. This is rather a natural consequence of the arguments above.

The market mechanism is, as has been discussed, not perfect, but rather quite deficient. The concept of solidarity is being proposed in this book as a unifying idea to seriously supplement the workings of the market. Solving social concerns and problems that urgently need to be addressed should become our very

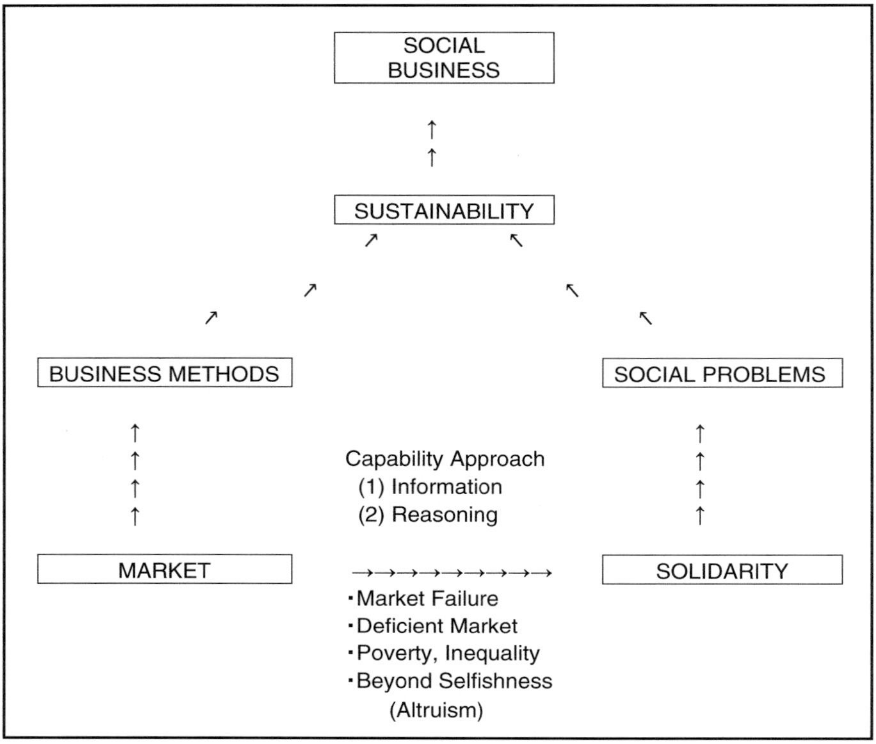

Fig. 1.1 Conceptualization of solidarity economy (market, solidarity, and social business)

first priority. There are a wide variety of social issues that society should tackle with the genuine and serious intention of solving such as poverty and inequality; food, nutrition, and safe water; energy resources and power supply; education and literacy; empowerment of women, minorities, and the neglected; organic agriculture; fair trade; environmental protection and promotion; revitalization of the local economy; and so forth.

In order to overcome the shortcomings of the market mechanism as revealed by intensified globalization which has brought about a very skewed and one-sided world economy, the idea of the selfish economic man who is supposed to pursue self-interest only has to be abandoned in lieu of a more balanced and natural conceptualization of human beings, i.e., the altruistic human being. The capability approach of Amartya Sen to understand human beings emphasizes the important roles that information and reasoning play in achieving higher/better well-being.

Sustainability requirements naturally call for better utilization of the market. It is well noted that NPOs, NGOs, and private volunteer organizations face serious financial problems in between the private profit-seeking market and collective action by the public sector. Without subsidies and assistance from other organizations like the government sector or private charities, those organizations have been chronically confronting a lack of funds in many areas of activities. Not only is social business a solution for this funding problem of NPOs and NGOs, but social business has a good characterization: honoring human incentive to work for financial motivation. By utilizing managerial skills and work incentive, social business tries to earn extra profit as much as possible. The important restriction on the social business is that the profit thus earned has to be used to solve social problems.

Figure 1.1 shows the relationship in the solidarity economy. It clarifies the conceptualization of the solidarity economy by describing the trilateral relationship starting from *market*, and proposing *solidarity*, and then on that basis, moving to *social business*. It can be understood that the relationship described here fits in the scheme of dialectic development.

The rest of this book discusses various social issues and concerns that have been grappled with in the form of social business in the world. It is hoped that social business will be used more and that we will learn better ways to solve many social problems and common questions.

1.6 Further Considerations

- Economics assumes selfish economic men. Consider whether altruistic people can achieve better results than economic men.
- When you answer the previous question, what do you mean by the word "better"? Is it "economically better," "socially better," or any other meanings?

References

Arrow KJ (1951) Social choice and individual values (1963), 2nd edn. Yale University Press, London
Robbins L (1932) An essay on the nature and significance of economics science. Macmillan, London
Sen A (1999) Development as freedom (2001), 2nd edn. Oxford University Press, New York
Sen A (2009) The idea of justice. Harvard University Press, Cambridge
Smith A (1759) The theory of moral sentiments (2002). Cambridge University Press, Cambridge
Smith A (1776) An inquiry into the nature and causes of the wealth of nations (1982). University of Chicago Press, Chicago
Wilkinson R (2009) The impact of inequality. The New Press, New York; Routledge, London

Chapter 2
Microcredit, Inclusive Finance and Solidarity

Noriatsu Matsui and Hiromi Tsuboi

Abstract The Grameen Bank of Bangladesh is one of the largest and most successful microcredit organizations. Its success in poverty alleviation comes from the human and organizational principles based on the philosophy of its founder, Muhammad Yunus. These Principles are embodied in Grameen Bank's organizational structure, the emphasis of weekly Center meetings, and above all the people-centered Sixteen-decisions. The meetings have served as education, communication, information, and social training for the poor who have never had such opportunities. Social business has been advocated and promoted as the mechanism to generate IGAs for the poor to use the microcredit. Social business and microcredit have been shown to be effective for the economic independence of the poor. Microcredit organizations pioneered earlier have led the development in this area in increasing financial access to the poor of the world, and various other financial activities, such as saving accounts, deposit accounts, insurances, and pension plans. Recent development from microcredit has evolved into inclusive finance, responsible investment, and assistance to the variety of social business.

Keywords Microcredit · Microfinance · Grameen Bank · BRAC · Poverty alleviation · Social business · Inclusive finance · Responsible investment

2.1 Introduction

This chapter discusses principles and development of microcredit. Microcredit system has become well recognized among development scholars, practitioners, and policy makers as a tool that is effective for the purpose of poverty reduction in

N. Matsui (✉)
Teikyo University, 359 Otsuka, Hachioji, Tokyo 192-0395, Japan
e-mail: noripmat@main.teikyo-u.ac.jp

H. Tsuboi
Graduate School of Engineering and Resource Science, Akita University,
1-1 Tegata, Gakuen-Machi, Akita 010-8502, Japan
e-mail: tsuboi@gipc.akita-u.ac.jp

N. Matsui and Y. Ikemoto (eds.), *Solidarity Economy and Social Business*,
SpringerBriefs in Economics, DOI 10.1007/978-4-431-55471-4_2

many developing countries. The system of microcredit has unique and significant relevance in development economics. It is unique in the sense that it is the only development mechanism which has originated in the developing world. It is significant because it is the system in which the wish and intents of the poor people are directly honored and utilized when it is successful (Smith and Thurman 2007; Ahmed and Hakim 2004).

Microcredit and micro-finance have been used interchangeably recently. When the term micro-finance is emphasized, it has been used to include more comprehensive financial activities than just giving credit to the poor. It includes savings accounts and other diverse financial activities beyond granting small loans to the poor. Deposit accounts, kinds of insurance, and housing and education loans for low income people are all included in microfinance activities (de Aghion and Morduch 2005).

It is estimated that there are 2.7 billion adults who do not have any access to banking services in the developing world. As mentioned above, microfinance recently has shown a remarkable track record as an important tool for fighting against poverty and has entered the financial mainstream the world over. Around 15–20 years ago there were very few microcredit organizations anywhere. The increase in the number of microfinance institutions in the world has been quite impressive. There are also so many wholesale institutions for microfinance that have sprung up that it is hard to imagine that Muhammad Yunus has been strongly advocating the necessity of establishing wholesale financial institutions for microcredit for poverty alleviation then (APO 2006; Mosley and Steel 2003).

In this chapter we will examine Grameen Bank of Bangladesh as a pioneer of microcredit for the poor in the developing world. Some of the characteristics in the operation of the Grameen Bank are explained in Sects. 2.2 and 2.3, after discussing a brief history of microcredit development. All the major factors and operational modes of microcredit are listed. Grameen Bank as the mother of social business for poverty elimination will be discussed as a form toward solidarity economy in Sect. 2.4. The next section, Sect. 2.5 surveys recent movements in this area of inclusive finance and various institutions' functions in providing a variety of financial services to the poor in the world. This chapter tries to capture the most influential and contributing elements and factors for the success of microcredit systems in the world today.

2.2 Development of Microcredit

The Grameen Bank of Bangladesh started to give credit to the poor in 1976. After significant struggle, it was established as a government-chartered bank in 1983. Today, the Grameen Bank services more than 8.5 million people in Bangladesh, loaning small amount of money to the poor with a repayment rate of over 98 %. The small amounts of credit are extended without any collateral to the poor who are normally refused access to formal banking opportunities. This method of giving credit to the poor has been so successful that more than 60 countries the world over have adopted this system of providing group-based, small amount of credit without any mortgage for the purpose of helping the poor escape from the trap of poverty and establishing their independence and thus their self-esteem (Khandker 1998).

Microcredit for the purpose of poverty elimination is a means to give leverage to the poor. The poor traditionally has been refused complete access to the banking system. Microcredit is intended to be useful in expanding people's substantial freedom (Sen 1999, pp. 39, 201–203), which is the ultimate goal of "development" and also is the means to achieve the development.

In a practical sense, the empowerment of the poor also requires instilling self-determination of their own life, and ability to organize, and thus resulting in self-confidence and self respects. Microcredit system designed for poverty elimination explicitly recognizes those important aspects put into the system. The borrowers in the microcredit system are encouraged to unite, attain mental independence, and to become able to manage their own resources with their own will free of external control.

In order to borrow money from the Grameen Bank, one has to become a member of a group of five. To be a member one has to be poor, own less than half an acre of land, and be able to write one's name by hand. A regular loan is given to a member who has to pay back the loan in 50 weekly installments with interest. Payments in weekly installments are done at the Center meeting, where not only payback and recording but also certain group activities are carried out. The group activities are very important for the rural poor because they constitute rare opportunities to get information from a wider world than they regularly would get to know, and to become educated in social life. Thus, Center meetings can be understood as a unique opportunity of adult education for the rural poor women.

After paying back the loan fully in 50 weeks, a woman can then obtain a larger loan again for another 50 weeks. These loans are supposed to be used for some income generating activities (IGAs) such as milking cows or raising chickens, fish farming, starting a weaving business, or similar small business activities for the family. How and when a borrower uses the loaned money depends wholly on the borrower, not on the direction or control of the lender, Grameen Bank staff.

Grameen Bank now has saving accounts, deposit accounts, pension programs, life insurance, and other types of loans such as housing, and business, and education loans. The growth and success of Grameen Bank has been attributed by number of factors. The loan recovery rate of higher than 97 % and the 96 % participation rate of women must be noted as significant because Grameen Bank operates only in rural areas of Bangladesh, one of the poorest countries in the world, and deals with women who usually do not have voices of their own in families and communities.

The organizational structure is shown in the Fig. 2.1. It should be noted that there are groups of Grameen members who are more or less than 5. There are also non-members who have deposit accounts, insurance policies, or pension programs now.

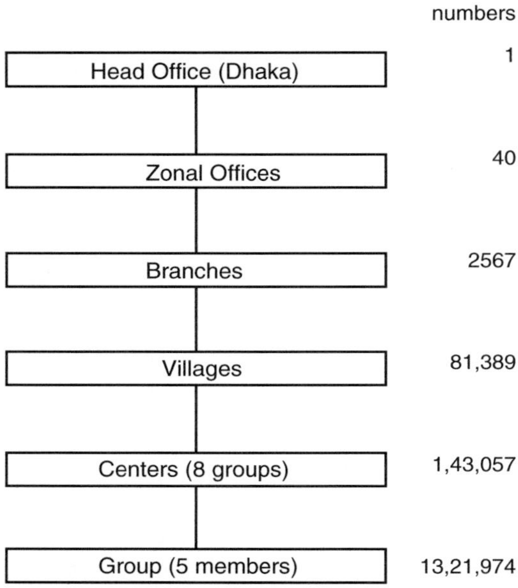

Fig. 2.1 Organizational structure of Grameen Bank. Numbers at right are from www.grameen.com, as of January 2014

2.3 Effectiveness of Microcredit as Social System

The purpose of this section is to discuss the nature and characteristics of microcredit as a social organization that under certain conditions functions as an effective mechanism to help promote the realization and development of individual capability. The discussion demonstrates how contributing factors for the success of the microcredit mechanism are much in line with human nature.

2.3.1 Grameen Bank

The basic activity of Grameen Bank is to give small amounts of credit to the poor without any mortgage. The following will list some of the fundamental features of the Grameen Bank's operation (Yunus 2007, 2010).

1. Credit to the poor, in small amount: In order to qualify as a member, one has to be poor, defined as a landowner with less than one half of an acre, or who is landless. The amount of credit given to individuals is approximately \$100–\$200 (i.e., about Taka 10,000–20,000, or in Japanese Yen 10,000–20,000).
2. No collateral: There is no mortgage, and neither is credit insurance required.
3. Group (5 members) based lending: Five members in a group all must be the same sex, and only one person from the same household can join in Grameen Bank. A leader of the group has to form the group voluntarily, based on trust. The formation of groups plays an important role in joint responsibility, because

only one member at a time can get the loan after other members start to repay in weekly installment.

4. Weekly installments: Repayment usually begins right after one borrows the money at the weekly Center meeting, in 50 equal installments including interest payment. The interest rate for a Grameen loan is about the same as that of commercial banks in the market, 18–20 % per annum.
5. Weekly meeting at Center: Center consists of up to 8 groups, thus up to 40 members. Bank workers visit each Center meeting, 2 meetings in each morning. One bank worker usually visits and attends Center meetings up to 10 a week. Center leaders and group leaders, working with a Grameen Bank employee, take initiatives to conduct the Center meeting and help the Grameen Bank employee collect the money.
6. No restriction on the use of the loan: each individual borrower can use the loan for any IGAs. For example, raising chickens, selling eggs, fish pond farming, buying cows and selling milk, weaving and yarn, and making dresses and clothes for villagers.
7. Strict principles and flexible practices: There are 16 decisions that members of Grameen Bank developed over the years. Grameen Bank has changed its organization quite flexibly to adopt new realities in the economy.
8. After some difficult times following the flood of 1998, Grameen Bank changed the entire system of lending the loan, depositing it, and making repayment more flexible. This is called the "Grameen Generalized System (Grameen II)" which started in 2002.
9. In 2004, Grameen Bank started the "Struggling Member Programme," which gives loans to street beggars.

Members of Grameen Bank at weekly Center meetings recite the 16 Decisions in order to remind themselves as a guideline for their daily lives. The *16 Decisions* of Grameen members are:

1. The four principles of Grameen Bank: Discipline, Unity, Courage, and Hardwork: we shall follow and advance in all walks of our lives.
2. We shall bring prosperity to our families.
3. We shall not live in dilapidated house. We shall repair our houses and work towards constructing new houses at the earliest.
4. We shall grow vegetables all the year round. We shall eat plenty of them and sell the surplus.
5. During the planting seasons, we shall plant as many seedlings as possible.
6. We shall plan to keep our families small. We shall minimize our expenditures. We shall look after our health.
7. We shall educate our children and ensure that they can earn to pay for their education.
8. We shall always keep our children and environment clean.
9. We shall build and use pit-latrines.
10. We shall drink water from tubewells. If it is not available, we shall boil water or use alum.

11. We shall not take any dowry at our son's weddings, neither shall we give any dowry at our daughter' weddings. We shall keep the centre free from the curse of dowry. We shall not practice child marriage.
12. We shall not inflict any injustice on anyone; neither shall we allow anyone to do so.
13. We shall collectively undertake bigger investments for higher incomes.
14. We shall always be ready to help each other. If anyone is in difficulty, we shall all help him or her.
15. If we come to know of any breach of discipline in any centre, we shall all go there and help restore discipline.
16. We shall take part in all social activities collectively.

Some of the Grameen Bank's principles are said to be that the right to get a credit is a human right, and that any human being has the willingness and ability to use the loan to improve their lives if the opportunity for a loan is given. These are based on the strong brief of Muhhamad Yunus. Therefore, Grameen Bank goes to the people instead of the people going to the bank. Referring to the situation that the poor were not given access to the credit simply because they are poor, Muhammad Yunus says that it is not that the people are not credit-worthy, rather that the traditional banks are not people-worthy.

Grameen Bank has adopted 10 indicators by which members are judged to be poverty-free. These indicators were developed over time, and not by imposition from the top of the organization but rather from people's need to identify poverty. A member is considered to have moved out of poverty if her family fulfills the following criteria. They are:

1. The family lives in a house worth at least Tk. 25,000 (twenty five thousand) or a house with a tin roof, and each member of the family is able to sleep on the bed instead of on the floor.
2. Family members drink pure water of tube-wells, boiled water or water purified by using alum, arsenic-free, purifying tablets or pitcher filters.
3. All children in the family over six years of age are all going to school or finished primary school.
4. Minimum weekly loan installment of the borrower is Tk. 200 or more.
5. Family use sanitary latrine.
6. Family members have adequate clothing for every day use, warm clothing for winter, such as shawl, sweater, sheets, blankets, etc. and mosquito-nets to protect themselves from mosquitoes.
7. Family has sources of additional income, such as vegetable garden, fruit-bearing trees, etc., so that they are able to fall back on these sources of income when they need additional money.
8. The borrower maintains an average annual balance of Th. 5,000 in her savings accounts.
9. Family experiences no difficulty in having three square meals a day throughout the year, i.e., no member of the family goes hungry any time of the year.
10. Family can take care of the health. If any member of the family falls ill, family can afford to take all necessary steps to seek adequate health care (Fig. 2.2).

Fig. 2.2 A scene of a weekly center meeting of Grameen Bank, Noyonpur Village, August 2007

2.3.2 *BRAC*

BRAC (formerly Bangladesh Rural Advancement Committee) is another known microcredit organization based on as "credit plus" approach. It was established as a relief and rehabilitation organization in 1972 after the Bangladesh Liberation War. Over the years, BRAC has gradually evolved into a large and multifaceted development organization with the twin objectives of alleviation of poverty and empowerment of the poor (http://microfinance.brac.net).

It has been very successful in extending loans to the poor in the rural areas and repayment rate is 97.97 %. At the end of 2003, BRAC covers all of 64 districts of Bangladesh, 94 % of Upazilas (480 out of 507). The members (they call Village Organization Members) are more than 5.66 million with 99 % of who are women in 282,412 Village Organizations over the country. BRAC has also established *18 Promises* for the members to recite at each VO meetings. They are;

1. We will not adopt corrupt or unlawful means.
2. We will work hard and improve our living conditions.
3. We will educate our children.
4. We will adopt family planning measures and have a small family.
5. We will keep ourselves, homes and surroundings clean.
6. We will always drink potable water.
7. We will always cover our food and wash our hands before eating.
8. We will build sanitary latrines & stop indiscriminate defecation.
9. We will cultivate vegetables around our homesteads and plant trees.
10. We will always help others.
11. We will fight against polygamy and violence towards women.
12. We will be loyal to our Village Organizations and obey its rules and regulations.

13. We will not sign anything without full understanding what is written.
14. We will attend the weekly and monthly meetings punctually.
15. We will obey the decisions of our Village Organizations.
16. We will deposit our weekly savings regularly.
17. We will repay all loans in time.
18. We will give equal opportunities to girls as well as boys.

2.3.3 Factors for Success

There are varieties of microcredit organizations not only in Bangladesh but also in many other developing countries. From many successful experiences, it is possible to extract the factors which have played critically important roles in microcredit systems that have served social organization for the cultivation and development of individual capability of the members of microcredit system.

First, there is an incentive mechanism to repay the loan fully. The rules of repayment and installment are simple to understand and easy to actually implement. Once fully paid back by a regular fixed number of installments, one becomes eligible to get a bigger amount of loan. A small group-based borrowing mechanism plays the role of mutual guarantee within the group. This mechanism is important because it works as the collateral which microcredit usually does not require, and because it prevents moral hazards from happening by requiring voluntary formation of the groups. Further evidence of the effectiveness of small groups is shown by higher default rates in the programs like the BRDB (Bangladesh Rural Development Board, a branch under the Ministry of Agriculture) microcredit program in which the number of group members is allowed to be 12–24. Having the number of group members near or more than 20 may often create free-riders and reduced incentive to repay regularly and ultimately even a borrow-and-run phenomena among the members.

Secondly, regular meeting attendance is mandatory not only for repayment but also for educating members and information dissemination. The role of education is quite significant in the sense that it gives the opportunity to raise awareness and literacy, to learn new things, to discipline punctuality, and also to train leadership in groups and among larger organization. Those who successfully show leadership qualities in small groups will be given further opportunities to become leaders in larger meetings. The role of information dissemination plays a significant role in order to widen the scope of knowledge on the side of the poor about family planning, nutrition, health care, housing, and children's education.

The third factor would be the fact that there is no specific requirement or specification imposed by the lender as to the use of the borrowed loan. This has often been one of the criticisms of Grameen Bank, suggesting that loans borrowed by women have been used up by husbands, that the loans can be used as means to repay other loans, and that there is no guarantee that the money is used for income-generating activities. Based on trust, microcredit utilizes and is dependent on the willingness and ability on the side of the borrowers, the poor, in terms of their capability to improve their own lives, livelihood and the overall quality of life including their children. So far, the evidence shows that it is effective to trust people rather than distrust.

Year 2005 was the UN International Year of Microcredit in which targets of the microcredit were to reach millions of the poor in the world and through which the target of halving poverty in the UN Millenium Development Goals (MDGs) can be achieved. In order for the system of microcredit to be successful it is necessary that adopts three aspects mentioned above with careful consideration of local conditions.

2.4 Grameen Model of Social Business as Solidarity

One of the ideas of Muhammad Yunus behind the system of microcredit is the brief that the poor is a natural entrepreneur. In other words it says that anybody and everybody can have chance to become a successful entrepreneur. All that they need is a bit of success in what they do and a small initial amount of money. The Grameen Bank believes that by lending that small amount of initial money in the form of a loan the poor can realize great potential to be successful in their life and business.

Banerjee and Duflo (2011) point out that there are two reasons why the poor tends to find better chance to be successful. One relates to opportunity (2011, Chap. 9). The poor have a better chance to get fresher and newer ideas that no one has tried, to the extent that they have not been given opportunities so far. The second reason recognizes a new development. The market has neglected the BOP (Base of the Pyramid). Now, the new innovations to improve the life of the poor are in the hand of the poor themselves.

In order to make people acquire a long-term perspectives, not only income alone but also a sense of stability may play an important role. The sense of stability means the sense of affirmation of controlling power over one's future through the recognition that one can get a stream of income every month for sure.

Muhammad Yunus of Yunus Center (formerly the Managing Director of the Grameen Bank) has been persuading the youth in the world to create "social business" to tackle various social problems in each region and country. Social business has been proposed as a viable form of enterprise to pursue the social problems. It is recognized that those social problems are the kinds which neither government nor private organizations can continuously deal with to achieve the purpose of solving problems in society for longer and sustainable ways.

The definition of "social business" has been proposed in quite different ways by various agencies and organizations the world over. Social enterprise, social entrepreneurship, and other terms were frequently used. The forms of business organizations also differ in the areas and scope of goods and services they offer.

However, it seems that at least two conditions are clearly commonly mentioned for the qualification as "social business." They are;

1. Solving one or more social problems must be the main purpose, therefore, even if profit or dividends are yielded, they will not be distributed to those who provided the capital.
2. The organizational management takes the form of business. This is so because it pursues the sustainability of the operation. Depending on donations, charity money, governmental subsidies, or even members' fees do not guarantee to sustain the operation. Independent and self-sufficient operation of the enterprise is the basis for this.

Notes derived from the first condition are (1) that profit, surplus, or retained earnings must be used to expand the operation, (2) that these extras must be distributed to the workers in the operation, or (3) that these profits may be utilized for establishing new business entities for solving social problems, in the form of social business. The principle of non-distribution of extra profits to those who provided initial capitals can be relaxed only in the cases of transferring to a fund or funds for social business investment. It may be noted that this point may be controversial in the definition and functions of social business. It may also be mentioned that this controversy has been developing since the early times of discussions of social business and also it depends on actually who and what organization is arguing as to the requirements to be classified as social business.

Yunus (2007, 2010) clearly describes the fundamental philosophy of social business. His general ideas are shown in the following:

1. The concept of social business is based on a broad framework, including microcredit.
2. A social business is a cause-driven company.
3. Therefore, a social business is defined as that which is not a charity but a company designed to pursue specific social goals by using business methods.
4. Social business is categorized into two kinds. One is a non-loss and non-dividend company owned by owners and investors, and the profits are reinvested to expand the company's reach and improve the product/service. The investors can only get back their original investment amount. This kind of company is called a Type I social business. Grameen Shakti (Energy), Grameen Danone Foods, and Grameen Veolia Water discussed in Chaps. 4–6 respectively come under this type. The other is a profit-making company owned by the poor directly or indirectly. Since all profits are plowed back into the poor, a company can alleviate poverty. Such a case is called a Type II social business. Grameen Bank, which is owned by the poor, is the only one example of this kind of social business, so far.

As for a Type I social business, Yunus presents his philosophy by the seven principles. They are:

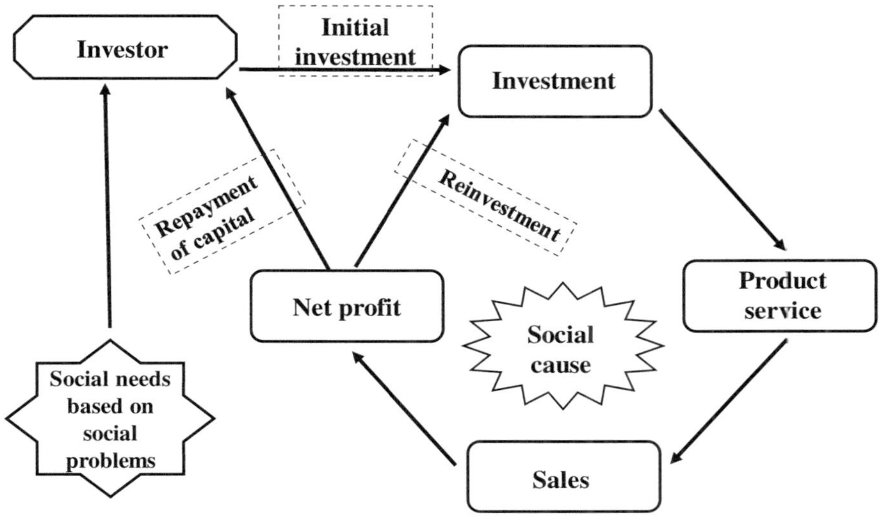

Fig. 2.3 Social business model of Type I

1. The business objective is to overcome poverty, or one more problems (such as education, health, technology access, and environment) that threaten people and society—not to maximize profit.
2. The company will attain financial and economic sustainability.
3. Investors get back only their investment amount. No dividend is given beyond the return of the original amount of investment.
4. When the investment amount is paid back, profit stays with the company for expansion and improvement.
5. The company will be environmentally conscious.
6. The workforce gets market wage with better than the standard working condition.
7. Do it with joy!!!

Figure 2.3 above summarizes the general ideas and seven principles, and illustrates Type I model of social business.

2.5 Credit, Inclusive Finance, and Recent Development

Recent development indicates that the microfinance instead of "microcredit" has been used quite frequently in order to capture the widening coverage of financial activities for the poor, and that inclusive finance is becoming a new key word for the changing trend in this area (Cull et al. 2013). The latter is most preferred as the term to show and deal with access to banking and financial opportunities in many parts of the world, not just developing countries and the poor.

The use of 'credit' was adamantly adhered to by the Grameen Bank administration because the term connotes the people's mutual trust and help in supporting the system. It is believed that whichever terms "microcredit (MC)" or "microfinance (MF)" is used, the important features of the organizations are members' trust, people's initiatives, and willingness to make the mechanism to work.

Instituting the system of lending small loans to the poor in the mechanism in which these principles are equipped and people's sense of mutual trust is honored has been shown to be very critical for successful operation in the thirty years history of microcredit.

In the following, we discuss some international organizations and effort to provide microfinance to the poor in the world (Shariff and Wood 2001). IFC (International Finance Corporation, World Bank Group) is a wholesaler of microfinance that it reaches more than 100 microfinance institutions in over 60 countries. IFC has been working with mostly private financial sector development. It underscores the importance of sound development of financial markets particularly for small and medium size enterprises.

CGAP (Consultative Group to Assist the Poor) was established in 1995 and now housed in the World Bank building. It functions as a coordinating organization among microfinance institutions (MFIs) and recently has begun programs of human resource development for the microfinance field. Its role of networking extends to many MFIs.

UNCDF (United Nations Capital Development Fund) and UNPRI (United Nations Principles for Responsible Investment) are two organizations we mention here. The former has worked since 1975 mainly in Africa for funding infrastructure finance, but gradually its emphasis had moved more towards inclusive finance and local development funding in the developing world. The latter is an organization that promotes principles of responsibility in investment projects.

2.6 Further Considerations

- Consider a name and mechanism of an organization to lend money, assuming that you are assured some fund. What other banking, non-banking, and non-monetary activities would you like to offer to your borrowers?
- Consider to create a new business in your area, or in your country to attack a problem you are the most concerned about assuming you were to receive funding. What social problem, kind and type, do you like to see solved?

References

Ahmed S, Hakim MA (eds) (2004) Attacking poverty with microcredit. University Press Limited, Dhaka

APO (2006) Regulatory architecture for microfinance in Asia. Asian Productivity Organization, Tokyo

Banerjee AV, Duflo E (2011) Poor economics: a radical rethinking of the way to fight global poverty. PublicAffairs, New York

Cull R, Demirguc-Kunt A, Morduch J (eds) (2013) Banking the world: empirical foundations of financial inclusion. The MIT Press, Cambridge

de Aghion, BA, Morduch J (2005) The economics of microfinance. MIT Press, Cambridge

Khandker SR (1998) Fighting poverty with microcredit: experience in Bangladesh. Oxford University Press (the World Bank), New York

Mosley P, Steel L (2003) Microfinance, poverty and social exclusion in north and south. In: Mosley P, Dowler E (eds) Poverty and social exclusion in north and south: essays on social policy and global poverty reduction. Routledge, London

Sen A (1999) Development as freedom. Alfred A. Knopf, New York

Sharif I, Wood G (eds) (2001) Challenges for second generation microfinance: regulation, supervision and resource mobilization. The University Press Limited, Dhaka

Smith P, Thurman E (2007) A billion bootstraps: microcredit, barefoot banking, and the business solution for ending poverty. McGraw-Hill, New York

Yunus M (2007) Creating a world without poverty. PublicAffairs, New York

Yunus M (2010) Building social business: the new kind of capitalism that serves humanity's most pressing needs. PublicAffairs, New York

Chapter 3
Grameen-Model Microcredit in a Developed Country: Spain

Hiromi Tsuboi and Nazrul I. Chowdhury

Abstract The Foundation ICO Microcredit Pilot Project is a Spanish microcredit institution based on the Grameen model. The purpose of this project is to alleviate social exclusion and financial exclusion, and to enhance social inclusion through the microcredit program. Before the banks offering loans merged, this project functioned quite well. This indicates that the Grameen model can be successfully replicated by microfinance institutions in Spain and address the needs of Spanish people. After the bank mergers, this project lost support from the banks that offered new loans to the project members, causing the project to struggle with continuing its rate of success.

Keywords Social exclusion/inclusion · Financial exclusion · Microcredit · Grameen model · Foundation ICO Microcredit Pilot Project · Bank merger

3.1 Introduction

The practice of offering microcredit to borrowers in poor communities has been expanding within the European Union (EU) since the 1990s. The purpose of spreading microcredit practices has been to address the problem of financial exclusion that many people living in the EU face and to ultimately improve their financial situations. The label "financial exclusion" indicates that people are deprived of access to financial instruments and services. Financial exclusion is one aspect of social

H. Tsuboi (✉)
Graduate School of Engineering and Resource Science, Akita University,
1-1 Tegata Gakuen-machi, Akita 010-8502, Japan
e-mail: tsuboi@gipc.akita-u.ac.jp

N.I. Chowdhury
Microcredit Project (Proyecto Confienza), La Caixa, Carrer ARQUITECTURA 2-4,
L' hospitalet De Llobregat, Esc-B, 1º 3ª, 08908 Barcelona, Spain
e-mail: nazrulgb@yahoo.com

N. Matsui and Y. Ikemoto (eds.), *Solidarity Economy and Social Business*,
SpringerBriefs in Economics, DOI 10.1007/978-4-431-55471-4_3

exclusion,[1] an issue that the EU has been tackling. Thus, as a member of the EU, Spain has also made addressing financial exclusion and social exclusion a state issue.

According to the bank's website, the Instituto de Crédito Oficial (ICO) is a state-owned bank in Spain, attached to the Ministry of Economic Affairs and Competitiveness via the State Secretariat for Economy and Enterprise Support (http://www.ico.es/web/ico/home). It was created in 1971. As a state finance agency, the ICO carries out its activities with its own assets and treasury based on its legal status.

The ICO has its group composed of two entities: Axis and the Fundación ICO (hereafter the Foundation ICO). Axis was established in 1986 and is Spain's first venture capital firm (http://www.axispart.com/axis/what-is-axis/?lang=en). Axis finances the growth of small enterprises by providing them with equity or quasi-equity instruments. Since 1986, Axis has invested nearly €300 million in about 140 enterprises.

Foundation ICO was founded in 1993 to promote Spanish culture and the arts. Since 2003, Foundation ICO has been operated as a nationally oriented, not-for-profit, public sector foundation with independent assets. Its mission is to foster and promote microfinance development and alternative finance opportunities in Spain. To accomplish this mission, Foundation ICO supports and participates in various activities, in coordination with universities, saving banks, NGOs, etc. One of the collaborative projects Foundation ICO established is the Foundation ICO Microcredit Pilot Project. This Microcredit Pilot Project is the EU's only project based on the Grameen model at the time of writing of this book.

This chapter focuses on the Foundation ICO Microcredit Pilot Project, and examines its activities and the feasibility of popularizing the Grameen model in Spain. The authors' own fieldwork serves as the basis for the following research.

3.2 The Establishment of Foundation ICO Microcredit Pilot Project

Many EU member states have specialized microfinance institutions to meet the large demand for small loans up to €25,000. Spain is no exception. Many Spanish financial institutions have started microcredit programs in order to provide financial support to the poor and to enhance their social inclusion. However, it is not easy for these institutions to keep a good balance between "non-financial support" and "financial support." Most microcredit institutions tend to give priority to providing small loans (Tsuboi 2009).

Considering this reality, Foundation ICO developed a microcredit program based on Bangladesh's Grameen Bank's fundamental philosophy. The program

[1] According to the Social Exclusion Unit in the UK, social exclusion is what can happen when people or areas suffer from a combination of linked problems such as unemployment, poor skills, low incomes, poor housing, high crime, poor health, and family breakdown (http://webarchive.nationalarchives.gov.uk).

takes into consideration Spain's social situation and integrates it with the Grameen model. As a result, Foundation ICO partnered with Foundation Cajasol, and established the Foundation ICO Microcredit Pilot Project in 2009. In 2010, Foundation Caja Navarra also joined this project, reinforcing the project's organization. The purpose of this Microcredit Pilot Project is to allow the poor to become more active in and to contribute more to their communities.

3.3 Target Beneficiaries

The Microcredit Pilot Project is made available to people who find themselves socially or financially disenfranchised and who are often looked down upon by other more "socially accepted" members of Spanish society. These beneficiaries commonly are:

- Female victims of domestic violence
- Those who have no vocational skills or are unemployed for a long time
- Those who are working for a minimum wage and for limited hours
- Those living in temporary shelters
- Immigrants (especially those who have difficulties with social and cultural integration)
- Poor single mothers
- Sex workers and ex-sex workers
- Romani people
- Ex-prisoners and ex-drug addicts
- Poor craftsmen

3.4 Basic Philosophy

In principle, the Microcredit Pilot Project implements and follows the Grameen model. The details of the basic philosophy are as follows:

(1) This project encourages members to form groups with a maximum of 20 people.
(2) This project is based on the belief that every human being has innate skills and potential.
(3) This project focuses on the poorest of the poor who are socially and financially excluded.
(4) This project focuses on welfare maximization of individual rather than profit maximization of organization.
(5) This project gives priority to non-financial support, though paralleling financial support.
(6) This project is based on mutual trust and good human relation. Therefore, it does not demand collaterals or legal procedures from members.

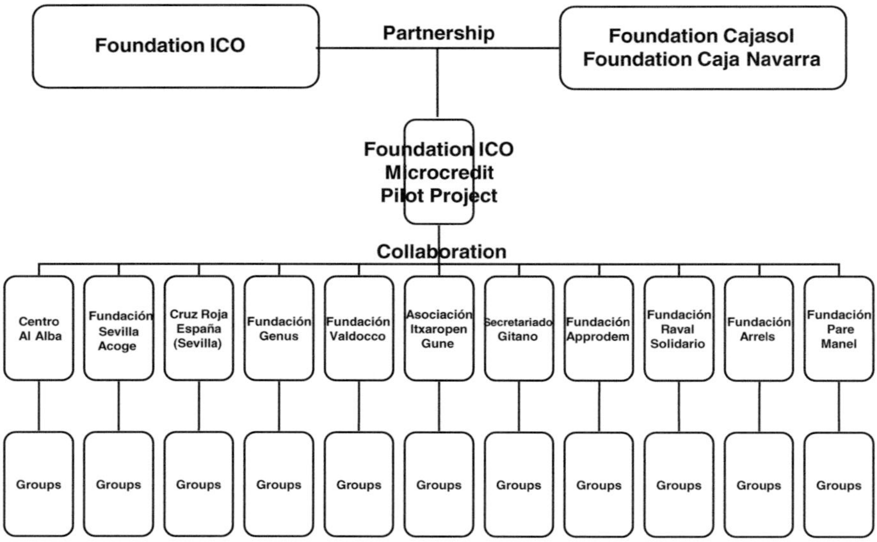

Fig. 3.1 Organization of Foundation ICO Microcredit Pilot Project

(7) This project strongly maintains discipline among members.
(8) This project gives unskilled poor people priority over entrepreneurs.

3.5 Organization

Unlike all other microcredit projects in Spain, Microcredit Pilot Project encourages the poor and/or vulnerable people to form groups. The reason is that most of the vulnerable people tend to be excluded from the community and isolated, therefore encouraging them to form groups allows them to have a sense of social belonging. This project collaborates with other institutions when forming groups. On May 5, 2009, the first group was formed in cooperation with the Centro Al Alba. The members of the first group were sex workers and ex-sex workers. The second group was created in collaboration with the Fundación Genus. It was composed of female victims of domestic violence. Figure 3.1 shows this project's organization.

3.6 Basic Methodology and Activity

The methodology of Microcredit Pilot Project is: (1) making door-to-door visits to recruit members; (2) organizing the members into separate groups; (3) conducting group meetings regularly (every 15 days); and (4) providing group-approved loans to

Table 3.1 Loan types

	Trust loan	Personal loan	Self-employment loan
Purpose of loan	For any immediate needs	For any personal purpose except immediate needs	To start a new business
Upper limit of loan	€600	€3,000	€15,000
Repayment plan	Monthly installment	Monthly installment	Monthly installment
Duration of repayment	Maximum 1 year	Maximum 2 years	Maximum 5 years with a 6-month grace period
Interest rate	4.5 % per year	4.5 % per year	4.5 % per year
Loan use	To open a bank account, application expenses to get a residence status, etc.	To buy a refrigerator, a TV, a computer, furniture, a sewing machine, etc.	To start a bread and cake business, a café, a grocery shop, etc.

Source Composed by the authors and (Tsuboi 2011)

members. It should be noted that although the group approves the loan, all responsibility for repaying the loan lies with the individual borrower.

The Microcredit Pilot Project provides members with two types of services: financial support and non-financial support (Tsuboi 2011). Three types of loans are provided under the financial support services: trust loans, personal loans, and self-employment loans (see Table 3.1). The project offers an interest rate lower than that of commercial banks, whose interest rate is 6–8 % per year. The project does not limit loans to small businesses. Loans can be used for personal, non-business uses such as coping with a state of emergency/disaster, and for buying household appliances or furniture.

The loan procedure is as follows:

(1) A member who desires to apply for a loan informs the group members of his/her intention at the regular meeting.
(2) A mortgage or a guarantor is not required, but the group's approval of the loan is mandatory.
(3) A designated person in charge along with an advisor conducts a screening. The advisor is a microcredit specialist with many years' work experience with the Grameen Bank, and visits the loan applicant at their residence for the screening.
(4) The person in charge prepares a formal loan application and submits it to the bank.
(5) The stipulated procedure is generally completed in 15 days.
(6) The borrower is advised to open an account with a specified bank (the Cajasol Bank or the Caja Navarra Bank), because both banks offer a loan, into which the loan will be deposited.
(7) The borrower directly pays his/her installment to the bank.
(8) The project can easily monitor the repayment of the loan through the bank.

Aside from financial support, the Microcredit Pilot Project also offers non-financial support. There are three types of non-financial support: regular meetings, workshops and lectures, and training and recreational gatherings. The regular group meetings are fundamental to the project, and are held every 15 days. The collaborating institution provides the meeting room (see Fig. 3.1). At the meetings, a person in charge: (1) recites the project's philosophy in order to raise the members' awareness of their present situation, and encourage them to break the vicious circle of poverty in which they find themselves; (2) encourages participants to establish mutual trust and reliance; (3) supports participants in recovering their self-confidence and self-respect; and (4) grasps an understanding of members' problems and needs, which they then attempt to solve. All members are required to attend the group-member meetings, where they: (1) get to know each other and build mutual relationships; (2) choose a group leader from among themselves; (3) share and discuss a member's troubles and anxiety; (4) take a lecture by a specialist; and (5) apply for a loan (when necessary).

The next type of non-financial support is workshops and lectures. The project's workshops and lectures are specifically meant to address the members' needs. Topics include citizenship, resident registration, rights and duties, management of family finances, managing bank accounts and credit cards, first aid, etc.

The third type of non-financial support is training and recreation. Collaborating institutions provide the social skills training and job training. Accounting is a popular topic for job training while social skills training is often combined with some type of pleasurable event such as visiting a museum or watching a basketball game. These training topics and activities are chosen specifically to meet the members' needs.

Figure 3.2 shows the microcredit business model in Spain. This model was drawn up based on the fieldwork the authors conducted in March 2009 and 2011. It is clear that there is a considerable difference between this project and more generally practiced microcredit projects.

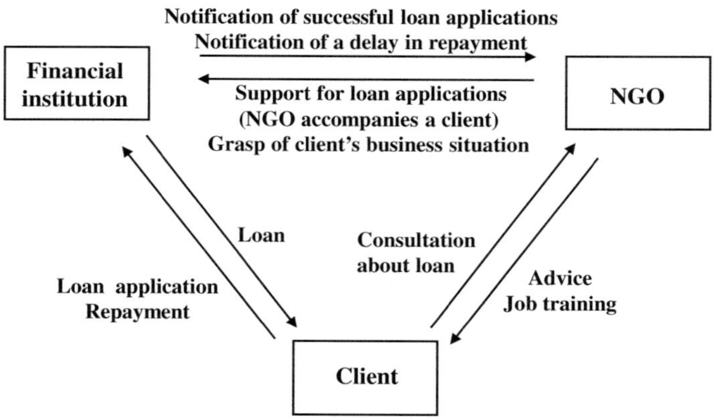

Fig. 3.2 Microcredit business model in Spain. *Source* Tsuboi (2009), p. 10

Table 3.2 Project performance, 2009–2013 (As of June, 2013)

Total number of groups		12
Total number of active members		244
Total number of group meetings		962
Total number of introductory courses/workshops		114
Total number of loans	Trust loan	51
	Personal loan	55
	Self-employment loan	12
Average loan size		€1,310
Repayment rate (*as of June*, 2012)		97.22 %

Source Internal Documents (Microcredit Pilot Project), calculated by the authors

3.7 Project Performance

Since the Microcredit Pilot Project launched in 2009, its success has led to expanding its performance (see Sect. 3.5). As of June 2013, (1) there are 12 active groups in four provinces (five in Sevilla, one in Huelva, three in Barcelona, and three in Navarra); (2) the total number of participating members reached 244; (3) group meetings have been held 962 times; (4) the total number of introductory courses/workshops reached 114; (5) the total number of loans is 118; (6) the average loan size is €1,310; and (7) the repayment rate is 98 % (refer to Table 3.2).

However, because of the acceleration of the banking bailout and reconstruction program begun by the Spanish government in June 2009, both the Cajasol Bank and the Caja Navarra Bank (see Sect. 3.6) respectively merged. As a result, neither of the banks could offer new loans to the project members in June 2012. The Foundation ICO cannot provide loans directly because of legal constraints, either. Recently, the Microcredit Pilot Project has limited its activities, although non-financial support is still possible, such as the regular meetings and some social activities.

Judging by the performance records reported above, it is noted that this project functioned quite well, and that the practical application (or replication) of the Grameen model to other microfinance institutions is a feasible solution to leveling the imbalance between non-financial support and financial support. However, given Spain's present financial circumstances, it is difficult for this project to manage itself as a microfinance project until it finds an alternative bank or similar institution that can supply the necessary loans for the project's members.

3.8 Further Considerations

- Consider the differences between Grameen Bank's method and the Foundation ICO Microcredit Pilot Project's method of building social capital.
- Consider the fundamental difference between microcredit and solidarity finance.
- Consider the repercussions of the Spanish financial crisis.

References

Tsuboi H (2009) Is microcredit in Spain a means or an end? Scientific and technical reports of faculty of engineering and resource science, Akita University, No. 30, pp 9–14

Tsuboi H (2011) Microcredit to include the poor among the community in Spain. Scientific and technical reports of faculty of engineering and resource science, Akita University, No. 32, pp 15–22

Chapter 4
Renewable Energy Resources for Villages Off the Grid

Hiromi Tsuboi

Abstract Low cost, renewable energy technologies introduced by Grameen Shakti to remote Bangladeshi areas appropriately suit the energy needs of rural Bangladeshis. Technologies that even the poor can access are highly sustainable and adaptable. Development of new technologies has clearly improved people's quality of life. First, due to these developments people can enjoy access to environmentally friendly renewable energy, as well as opportunities to generate more income. Second, demonstrations on how to use these new developments play an eco-educational role in society by creating awareness among the local people. Third, the new technology reduces the burden on women's lives, thus improving their quality of life. Moreover, training women both as engineers and as technology-users has empowered them tremendously.

Keywords Grameen Shakti · Solar energy · Biogas plant · Improved cooking stove · Women technicians and entrepreneurs

4.1 Introduction

Bangladesh is a country with insufficient electrical energy and gas supplies that cannot meet the demands of its population and growing industries. The electrical grid is slowly spreading throughout the country. Currently, only about 40 % of the population has access to electricity, with service mostly limited to those living in urban areas. Bangladeshis' energy consumption was 145 kW/h per capita in 2003 (UNDP 2006). In comparison, this was approximately 1 % of the United States'

H. Tsuboi (✉)
Graduate School of Engineering and Resource Science, Akita University,
1-1 Tegata Gakuen-Machi, Akita 010-8502, Japan
e-mail: tsuboi@gipc.akita-u.ac.jp

N. Matsui and Y. Ikemoto (eds.), *Solidarity Economy and Social Business*,
SpringerBriefs in Economics, DOI 10.1007/978-4-431-55471-4_4

total consumption (UNDP 2006). As for pipelined-gas, only a mere 3 % of the population enjoys access to it.

Due to the limitations of energy networks in Bangladesh, Grameen Shakti was established as a not-for-profit Grameen associated company in 1996 with the goal of improving Bangladesh's energy infrastructure (Barua 2005, 2006) (http://www.gshakti.org). At that time, the electric grid reached less than 20 % of the population and electric consumption was only 110 kW/h per capita per annum. Therefore, Grameen Shakti's mission has been to promote and deliver renewable energy and technology services at affordable costs to people living in remote and/or rural areas of Bangladesh. Grameen Shakti's integrated approach is meant to provide an effective strategy for reducing poverty and improving the quality of life of mainly rural people throughout the country. On December 6, 2010, the non-profit Grameen Shakti was registered as a social business in Bangladesh.

4.2 Overview of Grameen Shakti

Grameen Shakti has been playing a leading role in addressing and developing renewable energy programs in Bangladesh (Tsuboi 2007). It has applied its leadership expertise to a number of energy pursuits, but its main program is a solar energy program, which was Grameen Shakti's first challenging undertaking. Utilizing biogas technology and supplying homes with improved cooking stoves are also major focuses. While Grameen Shakti launches these programs, it also implements training programs conducted at the Grameen Technology Centers in order to popularize the technology amongst the people who will ultimately be using it. A list of all Grameen Shakti's energy programs appears in Table 4.1.

Grameen Shakti's performance is steadily improving. Evidence of this can be seen from the fact that by 2006 Grameen Shakti had programs operating throughout all the districts in Bangladesh. The biogas program and the improved cooking stove program also were launched in 2005 and 2006, respectively. As of March 2013, the total installation of Solar Home Systems and the total number of operational biogas plants are 1.09 million and 25,085, respectively (Table 4.2). To put the successful growth of the Solar Home Systems project and the biogas plants

Table 4.1 Grameen Shakti's energy programs

Renewable green energy technology (solar PV (photovoltaic) program)
Biogas technology
Organic fertilizer
Improved cooking stove
Grameen Technology Center (including training programs)
Tree plantation
Wind energy
Urban solar program

Source Kamal (2010, p. 19)

Table 4.2 Programs at-a-glance (*as of March 2013*)

Total office	1,507
(Branch office)	(1,264)
(Regional office)	(181)
(Divisional office)	(16)
(Grameen technology center)	(46)
Number of districts covered	64 out of 64 districts
Number of upazilas covered	508
Number of villages covered	50,000
Total employees	12,398
Total beneficiaries	Around 8 million people
Total installation of Solar Home System	1,092,578
Total number of improved cook stove	632,961
Total installation of biogas plant	25,085
Daily power generation capacity	243 MW-h
Number of trained technicians	16,614
Number of trained customers	443,840 users
Full paid customers (ownership)	267,458 customers
User under maintenance agreement (after 3 years)	34,151 customers

Source Grameen Shakti: At a glance, March 2013 (Accessed: April 22, 2013)

in perspective, it should be noted that Solar Home System installations and biogas plant construction increased to 13 and 50 times, respectively, between 2006 and 2012 (Tables 4.3 and 4.4).

4.2.1 Solar Home System

Grameen Shakti has developed the market based model for providing electricity to people who were once off the electrical grid by using solar photovoltaic (PV) technology. To create solar energy awareness among the people the program hoped to reach, an outreach program named Solar Home System was developed and promoted at the grass-root level. The program's solar PV system is a 12-V DC standalone system, including a PV module, a battery, a charge controller, and other hardware required for installation. As of November 2011, Grameen Shakti offers 16 types of Solar Home System models for sale. Most users choose the 20/21–50 W model, which accounts for 70 % of the sales performance. The cost of Solar Home System depends on the user's needs. Table 4.5 shows some examples of the package price of Solar Home System.

Grameen Shakti offers six types of payment options in order to better suit their customers' financial situations. Five of these payment options are soft financing options, and the sixth is a special option for the poorest customers, known as

Table 4.3 Installation of SHS (Cum)

1996–1997	228
1998	598
1999	1,838
2000	3,583
2001	6,753
2002	11,413
2003	19,213
2004	33,004
2005	51,646
2006	79,637
2007	127,976
2008	203,863
2009	317,599
2010	518,218
2011	755,672
2012	1,020,014

Source Grameen Shakti: At a glance, March 2013 (Accessed: April 22, 2013)

Table 4.4 Biogas plant construction (Cum)

2005	30
2006	483
2007	2,073
2008	4,621
2009	9,226
2010	14,906
2011	20,942
2012	24,206

Source Grameen Shakti: At a glance, March 2013 (Accessed: April 22, 2013)

the micro-utility system. Someone who purchases a Solar Home System via the micro-utility system rents his additional lamps to neighboring households or businesses. The neighbors who receive the additional lamps thus share the purchasing costs as well as the benefits that come with owning this resource. Around 10,000 customers participate in this micro-utility system. The six different types of purchasing options are shown in Table 4.6.

4.2.2 Biogas Program

In rural areas, Bangladeshis use cow dung, poultry droppings, and other biomass along with wood, bamboo, and hay as cooking-fuel. However, burning these materials causes indoor air pollution, which leads to ailments such as heavy coughing,

Table 4.5 Solar home system package price

Watt	Equipment supplied by GS	Package price
10	A 10 W panel, a 2/3 LED lamp or a 5 W CFL, an 18 A h battery, a charge controller, a frame, and cables	Tk.9,800
20/21	A 20/21 W panel, 2 × 5 W CFL or a 3 W CFL and a tube light, a 30 A h deep discharge battery, a charge controller, a frame, and cables	Tk.13,100
20	A 20 W panel, a 4 W LED lamp, a 30 A h battery, a charge controller, switch, and relevant accessories	Tk.20,400
30	A 30 W panel, 2 × 2.5 W LED lamp, a 5 W LED lamp, a 45 A h battery, a charge controller, switch, and relevant devices	Tk.22,300
40/42	A 40/42 W panel, 3 × 7 W CFL, a 55/60 A h deep discharge battery, a charge controller, a frame, and cables	Tk.23,600
40	A 40 W panel, 4 × 2.5 W LED lamp, a 5 W LED lamp, a 60 A h battery, a charge controller, switch, and relevant devices	Tk.33,500
50	A 50 W panel, 4 × 7 W CFL, an 80 A h deep discharge battery, a charge controller, a frame, and cables	Tk.29,500
50	A 50 W panel, 7 × 2.5 W LED lamp, a 5 W LED lamp, an 80 A h battery, a charge controller, switch, and relevant devices	Tk.43,000
135	A 135 W panel, 11 × 7 W CFL, a 100 A h deep discharge battery, a charge controller, a frame, and cables	Tk.72,900

Source Grameen Shakti: Solar home system (2011, leaflet)

Table 4.6 Solar home system purchasing options

Option	Down payment (%)	Installment (months)	Service charge (flat rate) (%)
1	35	12	5
2	25	24	6
3	15	36	8
4 (micro-utility system)	10 (20, 40, 50 W package)	36	5
5 (for worship places)	25	12	0
6	100 % cash payment with 4 % discount		

Source Kamal (2011) Best practice: the Grameen Shakti model (in preparation)

asthma, and other respiratory problems. Indiscriminate cutting of wood and bamboo by many rural residents has also led to deforestation in some regions.

In an effort to eliminate harmful indoor smoke pollution and to make rural people's homes more comfortable for cooking, Grameen Shakti took the initiative and began constructing biogas plants. Biogas replaces the traditional cooking fuels used for cooking and has the added bonus of being used for generating electricity. Yet another benefit to the rural inhabitants' local economy is that the slurry by-product from biogas plants is used as organic fertilizer material.

Grameen Shakti's biogas-plant promotional campaign involved representatives going door-to-door to publicize the biogas program and its benefits.

Table 4.7 Size and cost of biogas plants

Size (m^3)	Operational hours a day	Total cost
1.6	3–4	Tk.25,700
2	4–5	Tk.28,700
2.4	5–6	Tk.32,700
3.2	7–8	Tk.40,700
4.8	10–12	Tk.47,700

Source Grameen Shakti: Biogas program (2011, leaflet)

As of November 2011, Grameen Shakti offers two financing options for those interested in buying into its biogas plant model. Option 1 allows the buyer to construct a plant with his/her own funds under the supervision of Grameen Shakti engineers. For this option, half of the technical and supervision fees is to be paid in advance and the remaining half should be paid after the plant's installation. Option 2 allows the buyer to pay 15 % of the total cost as a down payment. The remaining 85 % is then paid in 24 monthly installments at an 8 % flat-rate service charge. Table 4.7 shows the various sizes and corresponding costs of Grameen Shakti's biogas plants.

4.2.3 Improved Cooking Stove Program

Approximately 90 % of the households in Bangladesh use traditional stoves (referred to as a "three-stone stove") for cooking and heating. People who own and operate these stoves use fuel materials such as cow dung, poultry droppings, wood, and straw. These traditional stoves consume about 44 million tons of the fuel each year and account for nearly 70 % of the total energy consumption in Bangladesh. For all the fuel they consume, these stoves are only about 5–15 % efficient. Apart from their low efficiency, the smoke from these stoves causes serious smoke inhalation-related illnesses.

In order to reduce the wasteful amounts of fuel these stoves consume and to curb smoke-related illnesses, the Bangladesh Council of Scientific and Industrial Research (BCSIR) started the Institute of Fuel Research and Development (IFRD). While keeping in mind the shape of traditional kitchen utensils and rural people's cooking habits, the IFRD has successfully developed a number of new stove models, or Improved Cooking Stoves, that are designed to consume biomass fuel more efficiently and cut back on harmful exhaust.

In cooperation with this initiative, Grameen Shakti has been distributing these Improved Cooking Stoves to those in need. The original stove was made of clay. This type had two problems: it took about a week to install and it was difficult to maintain the proper dimensions of the stove during installation (Grameen Shakti 2011).

In February 2010, Grameen Shakti developed new types of stoves that addressed these problems. Grameen Shakti's stoves are made of concrete and consist of five

Table 4.8 Price of improved cooking stove

Domestic improved cooking stove		Commercial improved cooking stove	
Single mouth	Tk. 760	Single mouth	Tk. 4,000
Double mouth	Tk. 890	Double mouth	Tk. 6,000
Double mouth for large families	Tk. 1090		

Source Grameen Shakti: Improved cooking stove (2011, leaflet)

Table 4.9 Growth of improved cooking stove (Cum)

2006	410
2007	4,998
2008	16,402
2009	45,967
2010	193,120
2011	423,725
2012	595,516

Source Grameen Shakti: At a glance, March 2013 (Accessed: April 22, 2013)

separate components: the base structure (for cooking), a chimney, chimney holder, grate, and chimney cap, all of which are produced in small, local factories. Grameen Shakti established a network of more than 100 Improved Cooking Stove production centers and has an army of locally trained technicians who can install the stoves in rural households within 1–2 h. As of November 2011, those interested in purchasing a stove can choose from between two options. One option is for those who want a stove for domestic use and the other option is for those who want one for commercial use. Both require a payment of 50 % of the cost beforehand and payment of the remaining balance after installation. Table 4.8 shows the prices of Improved Cooking Stoves and Table 4.9 shows the stove installations from 2006 to 2012.

4.2.4 Grameen Technology Center

Grameen Shakti established the first Grameen Technology Center in 2005. Since then, the number of technology centers operating in rural areas of Bangladesh has grown to 46 (Grameen Shakti: At a Glance, November 2011, leaflet). These technology centers employ female engineers. These female engineers train rural women, including young female students, as technicians and entrepreneurs. Through the Solar Home Systems, Biogas Plants, and Improved Cooking Stoves training programs, rural women learn how to assemble and repair the required accessories, install components, and maintain equipment. As of March 2013, the number of trained technicians is reported as being 16,641 (see Table 4.2). These technicians guide customers in the proper use and maintenance of these products. Specifically, the technicians are also training the women of the customers'

Fig. 4.1 A woman technician at the Grameen Technology Center

households in the proper use and maintenance of these products. These newly trained women of the customers' households then promote Grameen Shakti's technologies to other women in their communities by word of mouth (Fig. 4.1).

Grameen Technology Centers not only push for the sales of these new products, but they go one step further by advocating a better awareness of renewable technologies and environmental problems among rural people. In order to do so, Grameen Technology Centers offer education programs for not only rural school children but female students.

4.3 Impact on Rural People

Grameen Shakti's initiatives are truly having a positive impact on people's lives. Rural Bangladeshis participating in Grameen Shakti programs are enjoying a better quality of life. The programs have made their living environments, smoke-free, odor-free, cleaner, and healthier, with perhaps the most notable changes being made in creating more clean and comfortable cooking environments. Also, by making electricity available in more homes, families have been able to enjoy more recreational activities. Benefits of the participants in Grameen Shakti programs include the creation of new businesses and employment opportunities, both

Table 4.10 Impact on rural people

Income generating activities
• Lighting up homes, shops, offices, fishing boats, etc.
• Running computers, cellular phones, motors, etc.
• Extending business hours
• Creating or expanding businesses and employment opportunities
– Mobile phone shops
– Poultry farms
– Tailor shops
– Sawmills
– Cottage industries
– Electric appliance repair shops
– Solar lamp rental
– Tea stalls, etc.
• Training women to repair, maintain, and install equipment as well as training them to become engineers
Living environment
• Lighting up homes, schools, mosques, hospitals, etc.
• Operating TVs, cassettes, audios, small fans, etc.
• Extending children's studying hours
• Introducing comfortable kitchen work spaces, thus lessening the burden on women
• Reducing air pollution
• Improving the overall state of health
• Enjoying recreational activities
• Preventing deforestation

Source Classified by the author

of which generate more income for rural people. Grameen Shakti's innovation has also encouraged people to innovate. Take for example the mobile phone business—a new peripheral business that has sprung up. Entrepreneurs have used the Solar Home System to open solar-powered mobile phone shops and solar mobile-phone van shops. The former appears to be a typical shop, with the addition of the solar energy generators, while the latter is a rickshaw van equipped with Solar Home System providing mobile phone services as it is driven from village to village.

Table 4.10 summarizes the impact on Bangladesh's rural communities. The fieldwork conducted by the author for this study in November 2006, March 2008, and December 2011 corroborates this summary.

4.4 Further Considerations

- Consider the predominance of Grameen Shakti that accounts for 60 % of Solar Home System's installation in Bangladesh.
- Consider Grameen Shakti's activities from the standpoint of global warming.
- Consider and imagine yourself in a life without access to electric light.

References

Barua DC (2005) Grameen Shakti: an integrated approach to rural energy service. Grameen Shakti, Dhaka

Barua DC (2006) An introduction to Grameen Shakti. Grameen Shakti, Dhaka

Grameen Shakti (2011) A technical manual: ICS made of concrete. Grameen Shakti, Dhaka

Kamal A (2010) Paving the way for a green and sustainable future. Grameen Shakti, Dhaka

Tsuboi H (2007) Social business for poverty reduction: a case study of Grameen Shakti. Akita University no. 28, 31–35. http://air.lib.akita-u.ac.jp/dspace/handle/10295/459

UNDP (2006) Human development report 2006, 353–356, New York

Chapter 5
Yogurt for the Poor: Progressive Nutrition

Hiromi Tsuboi

Abstract The production, distribution, and sales of yogurt by Grameen Danone Foods have improved people's quality of life in Bogra. First, it has created new jobs and employment opportunities in the region as well as expanded previously established business. Second, awareness of Shokti Doi's nutritional value and its importance to people's diets has been promoted among local people. Grameen Danone Foods has been successful in creating this awareness due to the network of Grameen borrowers, workshops, and the weekly meetings held at the centers. The practical knowledge of the region's resources and of creating successful human networks is a result of Grameen Bank's successful practices over these three decades. As a result, rural Bangladeshi villagers enjoy the health benefits from Shokti Doi because of these socially conscious programs. And finally, because of this grass-roots program, nutritional education has been brought to rural regions, where healthier nutrition practices are much needed.

Keywords Grameen Danone Foods · Underweight children · Yogurt · Grameen Lady

5.1 Introduction

The Human Development Index (HDI) by United Nations Development Programme (UNDP) measures improvements made to people's quality of life. Particularly, the quality of life measurements are based on the improvements within

This chapter is a revised version of Tsuboi (2008).

H. Tsuboi (✉)
Graduate School of Engineering and Resource Science, Akita University,
1-1 Tegata Gakuen-machi, Akita 010-8502, Japan
e-mail: tsuboi@gipc.akita-u.ac.jp

N. Matsui and Y. Ikemoto (eds.), *Solidarity Economy and Social Business*,
SpringerBriefs in Economics, DOI 10.1007/978-4-431-55471-4_5

Table 5.1 Human development index trends in South Asia

	1975	1980	1985	1990	1995	2000	2005
Iran (Islamic Republic of)	0.571	0.578	0.615	0.653	0.693	0.722	0.759
Sri Lanka	0.619	0.656	0.683	0.702	0.721	0.731	0.743
Maldives	–	–	–	–	–	–	0.741
India	0.419	0.450	0.487	0.521	0.551	0.578	0.619
Bhutan	–	–	–	–	–	–	0.579
Pakistan	0.367	0.394	0.427	0.467	0.497	0.516	0.551
Bangladesh	0.347	0.365	0.392	0.422	0.453	0.511	0.547
Nepal	0.301	0.338	0.380	0.427	0.469	0.502	0.534

Source UNDP (2007), pp. 234–237

the areas of health, education, and purchasing power. Improvements in these areas lead to expanding opportunities for what people want to do and want to be.

Bangladesh has been making significant progress in human development during the last three decades. The HDI has recorded Bangladesh's human development growth and thus provides a standard measure by which future developments in Bangladesh may be compared.

As can be seen from Table 5.1, Bangladesh's HDI increased from 0.347 in 1975 to 0.547 in 2005. However, it is the second lowest in South Asia, and it ranks 140th among 177 countries (UNDP 2007, pp. 229–232). The index of underweight children under the age of five is one of the key indexes to monitor human development. According to this index, 48 % of Bangladeshi children under the age of five are underweight (Table 5.2). Not only does this indicate that Bangladeshi children in this age-range are in the poorest health in South Asia, but also in the whole world. Not only do young Bangladeshi children lack food for proper nourishment and growth, but they also lack access to healthy living conditions.

In order to make living environments of rural children in Bangladesh healthier, the Grameen Bank proposed to form a joint venture food enterprise between the Grameen Group and the French food company, Groupe Danone. In 2006, the newly formed Grameen Danone Foods began producing yogurt in the Bogra district, 230 km north of the capital, Dhaka (http://www.danone.at/fileadmin/

Table 5.2 Underweight children, 1996–2005 (% under age 5)

Iran (Islamic Republic of)	11
Sri Lanka	29
Maldives	30
India	47
Bhutan	19
Pakistan	38
Bangladesh	48
Nepal	48

Source UNDP (2007), pp. 238–240

template/Downloads/Press/DP_GrameenDanoneFoods_GB.pdf). The Grameen Group that formed this partnership with France's Danone Foods were Grameen Byabosha Bikash (Business Promotion), Grameen Kalyan (Welfare), Grameen Shakti (Energy), and Grameen Telecom. Grameen Danone Foods is officially registered under the Companies Act of Bangladesh. Their mission is to reduce poverty by providing a unique business model which will provide daily healthy nutrition to the poor.

5.2 Overview of Grameen Danone Foods

Four main objectives of Grameen Danone Foods are as follows:

(1) To offer a product with high nutritional value: Grameen Danone Foods produces a yogurt named Shokti Doi (meaning, "yogurt for power") which contains vitamin A, iron, zinc, iodine, and other micronutrients. As of February 2007, the price of each 80 g cup is Tk.5 (0.07 USD), and a single cup fulfills 30 % of children's daily nutritional requirements.
(2) To create jobs: Grameen Danone Foods also aims to help reduce poverty by buying their yogurt's main ingredients, such as milk and dates molasses, from local producers, providing plant jobs and involving communities in marketing.
(3) To protect the environment: the yogurt plant is operated by solar and biogas energy. Yogurt packages are recyclable and made using poly lactic acid which is created from corn starch.
(4) To be economically viable: Grameen Danone Foods is a company which implements a social mission based on a business model.

Grameen Danone Foods opened their plant on November 7, 2006. The total cost of building the plant was lower than the cost of a standard Danone facility. The plant's size is comparatively small with a surface area of 500 m^2. The plant optimizes the region's local resources. Where possible, it uses machines that do not require a lot of technical knowledge so that relatively unskilled employees can easily operate them. Most of the equipment, such as the boiler, air compressors, refrigeration equipment, gas generator, effluent treatment station, is all locally bought. Production capacity is 3,000 kg per day.

5.3 Distribution System

Yogurt must remain below a certain temperature so that it does not spoil, and thus requires refrigeration. Expansion of Bangladesh's electric grid to rural areas is extremely slow, leaving people in rural areas with either unreliable access to electricity or no access at all. Another point one must keep in mind is that most of the households in the rural areas are not even equipped with refrigerators.

Due to these circumstances, Grameen Danone Foods organized a clever and effective distribution system. In order to keep the yogurt chilled during delivery, factory workers put the yogurts in rickshaw vans equipped with ice boxes/coolers. The drivers then deliver the yogurt to "Grameen Ladies" (yogurt salespeople) and to designated shops within 5 km from the plant. The "Grameen Ladies" are door-to-door salespeople, who are also borrowers of the Grameen Bank. After receiving their yogurts, Grameen Ladies carry them in insulated blue bags supplied by Grameen Danone Foods and go out for door-to-door sales.

5.4 Workshops on the Product's Nutritional Value

The marketing strategy as well as the distribution system is tailored to the local conditions. Yogurt is popular among Bangladeshis, but is usually not nutritionally fortified. Bangladeshis do not traditionally consider yogurt as a nutritional supplement but rather as a sweet or dessert.

In order to challenge the traditional view of yogurt, Grameen Danone Foods holds workshops to create and heighten the product awareness (Yunus 2008). Through these workshops they publicize the fact that Shokti Doi has appropriate amounts of nutritional value and can make everyone, especially children, grow strong and healthy. As of March 2008 a traditional Bangladeshi yogurt sold in Dhaka and served in a big, clay cup cost between Tk.100 and Tk.180 (1.5–2.7 USD) per kilogram, which is much more expensive than Shokti Doi.

5.5 Impacts of the Program on the Rural Communities

The author conducted the fieldwork for this research during March 2008 at the following locations: the Grameen Danone Foods plant, the Mazhira Branch of the Grameen Bank, Center number 65 (one of the places where the Grameen Bank holds its weekly outreach meetings for borrowers), and Bejora Village in Bogra. The findings regarding the impact of this program are as follows:

(1) As can be seen from Table 5.3, Grameen Danone Foods' approach is to divide villages in Bogra into three blocks to which it assigns one sales manager per block (thus, three sales managers in total). The three sales managers organize a total of 54 Grameen Ladies. They employ one Grameen Lady per 1,000

Table 5.3 Sales performance by Grameen Ladies

	Sales manager (*n*)	Grameen Ladies (*n*)	Sales performance/block (cups/day)
Block A	1	20	1,000
Block B	1	18	1,000
Block C	1	16	1,000
Total	3	54	3,000

Source Author's hearings in the fieldwork

villagers. 1,000 cups per day are distributed to each block. The cups are then sold to the Grameen Ladies. Grameen Danone Foods fixes the allocation of cups for Grameen Ladies. There are three types: 50 cups, 100 cups, and 200 cups per day. Grameen Ladies can choose one of these three types.

(2) Most of the women selected to be Grameen Ladies already have some prior experience in door-to-door sales.

(3) Grameen Ladies earn Tk.1 per cup as a commission. They are supposed to save 30 % of this Tk.1. After one month of earning, they are free to withdraw their savings from their bank account. One Grameen Lady reported that she sells yogurt five days a week, selling 100 cups per day. According to her, she can earn Tk.2,000 per month, which supplements her regular income from another job she has. She said that it did not take a long time to sell out of her yogurts and that the best spots for sales were by the school gates as well as at the center (the place where weekly meetings are held).

Fig. 5.1 Grameen ladies (yogurt salespeople) with insulated *blue bags*

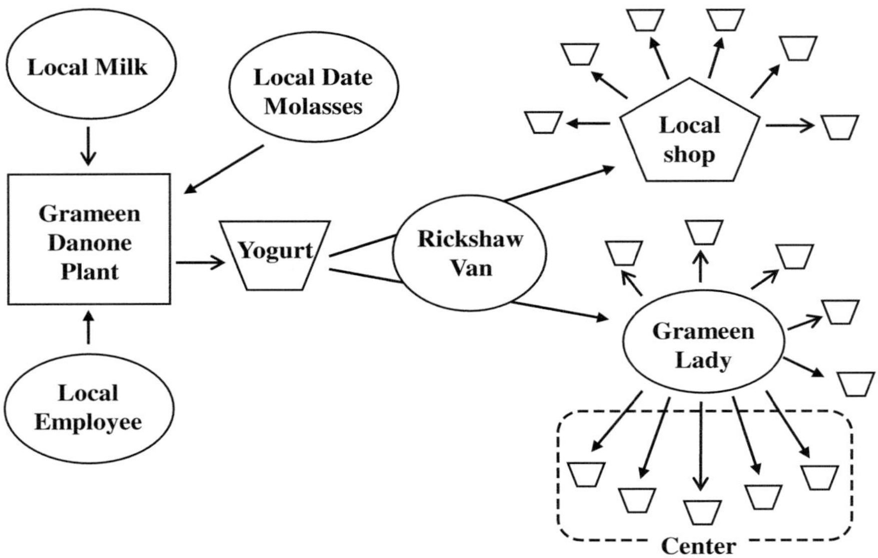

Fig. 5.2 Expanding income generating opportunities (Author's conceptualization)

(4) Local shops receive Tk.0.5 per cup as a commission, or half as much as a Grameen Lady earns.
(5) As mentioned above (Sect. 5.4), Bangladeshis consider yogurt as a type of sweet or dessert. To build awareness of the nutritional value of Shokti Doi, at weekly center meetings the bankers of the Mazhira Branch repeatedly explain the yogurt's nutritional value and the importance of a balanced diet. Grameen borrowers the author interviewed in Bogra mentioned that after tasting Shokti Doi they immediately recognized the differences in quality between Shokti Doi and traditional Bangladeshi yogurt. As a result, they now try to give their family members, especially children, two cups per week to supplement their regular diet.
(6) Local people (including Grameen borrowers) have enjoyed new employment opportunities or have been able to expand businesses opportunities as a result of this Grameen Danone Foods yogurt program (Fig. 5.1). For example, there are some male Grameen borrowers who used small loans called microcredit to buy rickshaw vans and started yogurt delivery businesses (Fig. 5.2).

5.6 Further Considerations

- Consider Shokti Doi's nutritional impact from the point of view of nutrition science.
- Consider the significance of Grameen Lady's activities within a cultural context.

References

Tsuboi H (2008) Yogurt for expanding opportunities: initiative of Grameen Danone Foods. Scientific and technical reports of faculty of engineering and resource science, Akita University, No. 29, pp 17–22

UNDP (2007) Human development report 2007/2008. UNDP, New York, pp 229–232, 234–237, 238–240

Yunus M (2008) Creating a world without poverty: social business and the future of capitalism, Subarna, Dhaka, pp 149–152

Chapter 6
Distributing Clean Water in Communities

Hiromi Tsuboi

Abstract Bangladesh has the largest population at risk of arsenic poisoning in the world. The groundwater in about 90 % of Bangladesh's 64 districts is contaminated with arsenic. In order to supply safe drinking water to the poorest communities of Bangladesh, Grameen Veolia Water launched a water treatment and distribution business. This company constructed a plant with 4 km of pipelines, and has been distributing safe drinking water by treating surface water drawn from the local river. This company has introduced a marketing strategy tailor-made to the needs of the plant's locale, and maximizes the Grameen network to create and spread awareness of the value of safe drinking water. Local women play an essential role in building social networks at the water tap locations.

Keywords Grameen Veolia Water · Arsenic poisoning · Surface water · Water supply system · Grass-roots water education

6.1 Introduction

Access to clean water is absolutely essential for a healthy, prosperous and safe life. Therefore, access to clean water should be considered a basic human right.

Bangladesh is a country with abundant fresh water. Most of the rural population used to consume water directly from ponds and rivers. In the 1970s and 1980s, nearly eight million tube wells were installed throughout Bangladesh. People began using groundwater pumped up from the tube wells, which now account for

This chapter is a revised version of Tsuboi (2010).

H. Tsuboi (✉)
Graduate School of Engineering and Resource Science, Akita University,
1-1 Tegata Gakuen-machi, Akita 010-8502, Japan
e-mail: tsuboi@gipc.akita-u.ac.jp

N. Matsui and Y. Ikemoto (eds.), *Solidarity Economy and Social Business*,
SpringerBriefs in Economics, DOI 10.1007/978-4-431-55471-4_6

almost 90 % of people's water access (Chowdhury and Gilbert 2008). However, due to Bangladesh's natural geology, most of the groundwater was discovered to be contaminated with arsenic. The Department of Public Health Engineering of Bangladesh first reported this contamination in 1993 (Rahman 2006). Studies by the World Health Organization (WHO) indicate that people drink water filtered through arsenic-rich rocks and that consuming this water causes all the symptoms of arsenic poisoning(WHO 2013). In March 2004, Bangladesh's government adopted guidelines met to curb the amount of arsenic in drinking water. However, the number of alternative water sources is limited and the supply of safe drinking-water still remains a crucial problem. Today, more than 30 million people face great danger of chronic arsenic poisoning which has often resulted in death (UNDP 2006).

In order to supply safe, arsenic-free drinking-water to Bangladesh's poorest communities, Grameen Veolia Water launched a water-supply business, which follows a social business model. The social business has attracted attention since the Millennium Development Goals were determined. Grameen Veolia Water is in the Grameen Group network. The Grameen Group has played a leading role in solving social problems in Bangladesh through their ongoing efforts to start up social businesses.

6.2 Overview of Grameen Veolia Water

In March 2008, Grameen Veolia Water was established as a social business joint venture between Grameen Healthcare Services, a Grameen Bank subsidiary, and Veolia Water AMI (Africa, the Middle East, and the Indian subcontinent), a Veolia Water subsidiary. Grameen Veolia Water is registered in Bangladesh.

Grameen Veolia Water initially planned to build five water treatment plants by 2012 and to provide 100,000 local people in about five villages. These water treatment plants would provide the people with drinkable water that was also suitable for their other essential needs, such as for cooking, at an affordable price. Grameen Veolia Water estimated the cost of building the five plants to be US$ 800,000. The investment would then be repaid by water charges levied on consumers.

Grameen Veolia Water constructed the first plant 50 km east of Dhaka in the poorest village of Goalmari Union in the sub-district of Daudkandi Upazila, (which is in Comilla District, Chittagong Division). The Bangladeshi government reports that more than 80 % of the groundwater from tube wells in the rural areas is contaminated with arsenic. Goalmari also has a number of arsenic-contaminated tube wells.

Water purification operations in the first plant started in April 2009. Thanks to Veolia's technical know-how, local business manufactured the equipment needed for the plant (except for pipes that were made in India). Since surface water generally is not contaminated with arsenic, the plant uses water from Meghna Gomti River. The water treated at the plant undergoes traditional antibacterial treatment

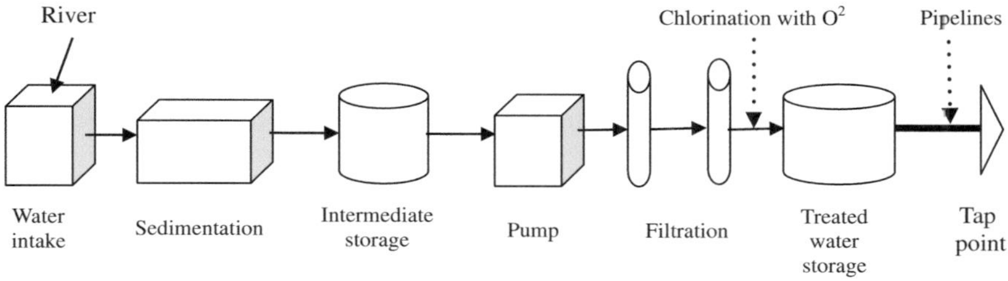

Fig. 6.1 Process of water purification. *Source* Grameen Veolia Water Ltd. (leaflet)

through activated carbon filtration and chlorination. Figure 6.1 shows the water treatment process.

As of March 2010, the first plant is in full operation. The plant's capacity is 10 m^3 per hour. The plant then pumps the water through 4 km pipelines to eleven tap points. The plant intends to supply water to approximately 25,000 inhabitants. The water is produced complying with the WHO's standards, which allows for 0.01 mg/l of arsenic in drinking water. Grameen Veolia Water and external laboratories such as International Center for Diarrheal Diseases Research, Bangladesh (ICDDR) and Bangladesh University of Engineering and Technology (BUET) regularly monitor and analyze the plant's water quality.

6.3 Safe Drinking-Water Awareness

In general, people in the rural areas of Bangladesh consider water to be free goods, meaning they should not have to pay for water. Target consumers of Grameen Veolia Water in Goalmari are accustomed to using groundwater and river surface water free of charge. They rarely, if ever, buy bottled water, which, for example, costs Tk.10–12 (0.15–0.18 USD) per 500 ml. The Bangladeshi government has recently installed 240 m-deep tub wells there allowing people to enjoy arsenic-free water (that is, within the allowable 0.05 mg/l range) free of charge, although bacteria in the water is not removed properly.

In order to address both the water-borne bacteria problem and the arsenic problem, Grameen Veolia Water has introduced a marketing strategy tailor-made to local needs. Specifically, Grameen Bank provides its intimate knowledge of the local region, and uses human networks to spread awareness of the health value of Grameen Veolia Water's water supply. Grameen Bank directly informs Grameen Bank's borrowers and other locals about what it means for water to be safe and why it is essential for people's health. Grameen Bank disseminates this information through workshops held for the local people that are conducted by Grameen Healthcare Services, as well as through weekly center meetings of Grameen Bank to which every Grameen Bank loan borrower is encouraged to attend. In addition, Grameen Healthcare Services puts up posters and slogan boards in conspicuous places throughout the villages. It also distributes school supplies to pupils/students in order to raise their consciousness about health and encourage them to pass along the importance of safe drinking-water to their parents, family, and/or guardians.

6.4 Impacts of Safe Drinking-Water on the People

The author conducted the fieldwork for this research at the first Grameen Veolia Water plant and a water point of Paschim section of Goalmari village, in March 2010. The findings of the fieldwork are as follows:

(1) As of March 2010 (ten months after the plant's inauguration), Grameen Veolia Water's treated-water reached 800 out of 3,500 inhabitants of Paschim-para.
(2) Water dealers (that is, tap point managers), who are recommended by the Grameen Bank, are recruited from among Grameen Bank's borrowers to supervise the tap points. Milon Begum is one of them (Fig. 6.2). She is in her forties with two sons and two daughters. She has been a member of the Grameen Bank for 20 years. She received a small loan from the Grameen Bank to run an engine boat business, and now earns Tk.8,000–10,000 (120–150 USD) a month.
(3) Water dealers undergo one-day-training to learn how to maintain a tap point and how to sell the water.
(4) In rural Bangladesh, the majority of village people cannot afford to install water pipes in their home. And if they could, a system of monitoring water consumption for billing customers does not exist. Therefore, the water-distribution system and the water-charge-collection system are tailored to the local context. Eleven tap points have been established in a rather densely populated area of the village, where the water dealers sell water to people who buy the water with tokens instead of cash. A token for five liters is round and a square token is worth twelve liters. These different shapes benefit the illiterate people, who from 2005 to 2008 made up 45 % of Bangladesh's population according to the *Human Development Report* 2010 (UNDP 2010).
(5) The water dealer position is a new job created by Grameen Veolia Water. These positions go to Grameen Bank's senior borrowers who are placed in this position of responsibility. Water is sold for Tk.3 per ten liters at the tap point, and the water dealers receive a commission of five *paisa* (Tk.0.05) per liter. In Milon's case, she gets Tk.50–80 per day as her commission, meaning that she sells approximately 1,000–1,600 liters a day. Since people's water consumption changes with the seasons, Milon's income from this side job also fluctuates throughout the year. As one may expect, water sales increase in the summer, and decrease in the winter. Grameen Veolia Water estimated that the daily consumption for a family of six is 30 liters per day (Chowdhury and Gilbert 2008). Suppose this estimation was used, Milon would have at least a total of 30 households per day as customers.

Fig. 6.2 Milon, a water dealer, at the water point

(6) Milon sells water from 8 to 10 a.m. and 5 to 8 p.m. every day. People, mainly women, gather around the water tap and enjoy chatting, exchanging information, etc. The space around the water tap is an important place for women to get together. Women are building social networks at these tap points.

(7) Grameen Veolia Water has been successful in creating awareness of the value of safe drinking-water among the local people. An indication of this success is the fact that village women other than those associated with Grameen Bank's programs have started buying Grameen Veolia Water's—no doubt as a result of the campaigns to spread awareness through ad campaigns and through reaching school children.

The information on Grameen Veolia Water's programs suggests that Grameen Veolia Water plays an important role in the rural residents' health, local economy, and in improving social capital. However, there are still a lot of rural Bangladeshis who do not have access to Grameen Veolia Water (about 80 % in Paschim-para's case). This implies that people still tend to drink the free groundwater (which may not be contaminated with high levels of arsenic but still has bacteria that are not removed properly) rather than pay for and drink water complying with the WHO standards. Moreover, according to the 2005 poverty line (which is based on Cost of Basic Needs, or CBN), rural residents of Comilla District are among the country's lowest earners, making about Tk.749 a month for each person (JBIC 2007). Since Grameen Veolia Water suggests that consumers use a minimum of five liters a day per capita, water cost may be up about Tk.45 per month, which accounts for 6 % of the monthly expenditure.

6.5 Further Considerations

- Consider the water cost from the point of view of the poorest households.
- Consider other safe-drinking-water sources that may prove to be more easily accessible to the poor.

References

Chowdhury S, Gilbert O (2008) Water treatment and cost recovery through social business of Grameen-Veolia Water Ltd in Bangladesh, 2. http://www.expozaragoza2008.es/ContenidosAgenda/tda/ST0536.pdf. Accessed 5 Mar 2010

JBIC (2007) Poverty profile of Bangladesh, 10. http://www.jica.go.jp/activities/issues/poverty/profile/pdf/bangladesh_fr.pdf. Accessed 29 June 2010

Rahman M (2006) International research on arsenic contamination and health. J Health Popul Nutr Int Centre Diarrhoeal Dis Res 24(2):123

Tsuboi H (2010) Safe drinking-water for the poor: initiative of Grameen Veolia Water Ltd. Scientific and technical reports of faculty of engineering and resource science. Akita University, No. 31, pp 21–27

UNDP (2006) Human development report 2006. UNDP, New York, pp 40–41

UNDP (2010) Human development report 2010. UNDP, New York, p 194

WHO (2013) Water Sanitation Health. http://www.who.int/water_sanitation_health/dwq/arsenic/en/. Accessed 2 Oct 2013

Chapter 7
Local Currency and Regional Revitalization

Noriatsu Matsui

Abstract Since the early 1980s a number of different designs for local currency system have been experimented with in the world. Some were quite successful in that a large number of people participated and some designated targets were fulfilled as a result of active exchanges of goods and services. At the same time, another large number of groups had tried, failed, and disappeared. Funding is one of the quite serious problems for many organizations. How to procure the necessary funding has not been an easy problem to solve. Who takes the initiatives in organizing the system, and for how long a period the organization should exist, are other really important issues that deserve serious consideration. It is worth while to point out some of the basic issues for successful local currency practices that can be observed from past experiences. The first point is about government involvement. It can be said that public administration should not be directly involved in local currency because this is based on initiatives and activities of private citizens. Public administration either local or national should play a supportive role if asked. The second point is to make the major purpose of the system clear from the beginning. In order to have the system of local currency run well for certain long periods of time, a clearly defined purpose and easy-to-see targets are vitally important. Not only should embracing the purpose and target be clear but communicating and widely disseminating them among the members is one of the key elements for a well-run organization. The third and final point is that it is important to realize among the participants that nothing comes automatically without spending lots of time and sweats by the people. Local currency mechanism is a system in which citizen's initiative and active participation are essentially important. Also important is the recognition of the fact that local currency is not a panacea for social ill or market failure, though it is an effort on the side of people to make the community in which they live more enjoyable to live together than today's globalized, isolated, and cold-hearted market economy.

N. Matsui (✉)
Teikyo University, 359 Otsuka, Hachioji, Tokyo 192-0395, Japan
e-mail: noripmat@main.teikyo-u.ac.jp

N. Matsui and Y. Ikemoto (eds.), *Solidarity Economy and Social Business*,
SpringerBriefs in Economics, DOI 10.1007/978-4-431-55471-4_7

Keywords Local currency · Regional money · Regional revitalization · Market failure · Efficiency · Poverty · Income disparity · Community development · Trust

7.1 Introduction

A local currency, or regional money, is a currency not backed by a national government (http://en.wikipedia.org/wiki/Local_currency). Therefore, it is not a legal tender, but rather it is intended to be used only as a means of trade within a small area or region. In its early use, the terms community money or ecology money were frequently used. They were expressions used for certain purposes among specific groups of people who share the specific values and needs of a small community or region in which transactions of goods and services were easily executed on a personal basis. These terminologies also express the groups' and system managers' intentions of creating money only as a means of transaction so that they would avoid the negative aspects of modern monetary economy such as income disparity and unequal accumulation of wealth.

In economics, money can be defined as something and anything that satisfies all three of the following functions; (1) a means of transaction, (2) a standard of value and measurement, and (3) a means of accumulation/preservation of value. Money can play extremely important roles in modern market economies. Two of the benefits of a monetary economy are reduced transaction costs and increased information that promote market dealings among people. However, it became increasingly apparent that the recent globalization of the world economy in every part of the world has revealed the inherent deficiencies related with monetary transactions in the market economy. Malfunctions, misfunctions, and non-working of markets have been seen rampant almost everywhere in the world. Market failures as well as government failures are recognized as not being able to be solved easily. In the mean time, income gaps amongst people are becoming wider, and so is the gap between the center of the economy and the local areas.

Thus, there have been different ideas proposed and various experimental practices relating to the local currency in many places of the world (Keynes 1936). Local currency can take various forms such as paper money, money formed into metal or plastic tips, or even just virtual numbers in an account. The actual form of money as a means of transaction adopted in the system of local currency can be determined by the group or system manager's consideration depending on the local conditions such as people's preferences.

This chapter examines the principles and roles of local currency for various purposes in relatively small regions in which oftentimes the major purpose of the local currency is to revitalize the local business activities through the means of the local currency. Local currencies have been created, used, experimented with, and revised in many parts of the world (Fisher 1932). Some have been successful in that the experimentation heightened awareness of the importance of regional/local business and of the vital necessity of cohesive policy for further actions in local economies without depending on central government support.

Some examples of the experimentation are introduced here. Based on these, conditions and environments for the successful implementation of local currency are examined.

The purpose of this chapter is to understand and illustrate the use of local currency as a means of creation and support for the solidarity economy in small areas without causing income disparity between the rich and the poor. One of the important features attached to local currency is that the money in the system is designed not to have the function of wealth creation and accumulation. Another feature sometimes emphasized about local currency is that people can attach different values even for the same commodity or services, yet the pricing is fully dependent on the mutual understanding among the participants and agreement, which is based on trust and empathy in the community.

7.2 Why Local Currency? Deficiency of MONEY

A market economy is said to achieve equilibrium when it is competitive. The equilibrium price and quantity determined in each market have some significance in that they are the expression of satisfaction of all the participants in transaction, i.e., both all the buyers and all the sellers, that the equilibrium price has stability characterization under certain conditions, that there is neither excess supply nor excess demand at the equilibrium, and therefore that all the economic resources are fully and most efficiently utilized.

Some conditions of this model of perfect competition must be applied for the market in order to realize all the benefits and significance of economic meanings mentioned above. There are at least five conditions that the market has to meet in order to achieve perfect competition. They are,

(1) There is a large number of both buyers and sellers,
(2) The service or product in a market is homogeneous,
(3) There is no single buyer or seller that can affect market price by controlling quantities,
(4) There is no externality, that is, no external economy or no external diseconomy in the market,
(5) All the information on the price, quality and quantity are known to any and all the participants.

While a market economy can have a number of advantages over other forms of economic systems, it contains within itself deficiencies that cannot be addressed properly. Sympathy to other people is one of them. In a pure market, there is no concern over what the other participants feel about the transactions. For example, as an economic man you do not consider whether the other side of the deal is from the wealthy or from the poor group or whether the other is male or female, young or the old, or is able to speak the same language or not. It is simply beyond consideration of the model whether ultimate buyers of a product or original producers/workers/harvesters of a consumer good that you consume are sick, one-parent families, or orphans.

The ideal model of perfect competition in a market economy does not consider the ways and means to achieve the possibility of human coexistence with either the environment or inequality. They are simply outside conditions and exogenous parameters that the model does have any direct concern within its own closed system. Even though there is a trend for more pro-environmental activities and discussions observed in various parts of world, they are taken seriously only to the extent that they promote short-term profit maximization of each enterprise and organization's maximum benefit.

Another serious defect of this model of market economy deals with information. Information is always separated, hidden, not all are opened, limited in its availability and access to everybody, and quite often only partially disclosed so that the public may be misguided. This is because not disclosing the information, giving only partial information, or even misrepresenting information is beneficial to the owners of information in the market. Of course, the depth and width of the information on a product held by sellers and buyers might be quite different. This is a well-known problem of information asymmetry and information costs.

As a result of these "deficiencies" which is inherent to the market economy, there are a number of serious issues of civil concern that have attracted people's attention. One would be the deterioration of local economies that are far away from the major centers of the national economies in advanced industrial countries. In many countries, urbanization of the land, and sprawling suburban development were rapidly progressed along with the development of transportation networks including highways, railroads, and air transportation systems. As a result, the gap between the limited number of centers of a national economy and the local economies, the periphery, has been experiencing a rapid widening in terms of economic and political power. The deterioration of the periphery, the local small regions has been becoming more obvious than ever in industrial countries. This widening gap between the center and the periphery may be even bigger in many developing countries than in industrial countries.

The employment structure in industrial countries has also been getting skewed. In theory, industrial structure must go hand-in-hand with the changing employment structure. In the theory of general equilibrium, all the markets, i.e., products markets and resources markets, should reach a state of general equilibrium. In both goods and services markets, and factor markets, prices are determined as a result of the interaction between demand and supply. The prices thus determined will affect and dictate the quantities. However, the changes in employment structure tend to lag behind the changes in industrial structure.

The next deficiency of the market mechanism is the world's poverty. The market does not deal with the problem of extreme poverty, particularly, widening degrees of poverty in developing countries. A state of income distribution is not a direct concern of the market mechanism itself. Whatever the state of income distribution, the income disparity, that the market economy has brought, is said to have significance for economic efficiency in terms of resource allocation in the economy. The efficiency that the market achieved has nothing to do with the states of income disparity and the degrees of poverty of the people in the market.

Not only the widening poverty in developing countries but also disparity and inequality in income distribution in industrial countries are becoming significantly larger. In other words, the disparity between "the haves and have-nots" has been observed as getting bigger, particularly with the rapid progress of globalization of the world economy.

Another problem with the market is the delayed formation of the middle class in a national economy. Emergence and formation of the middle-income group is accompanied by the transition of a national economy from the developing stage to the industrial stage. To the extent that industrial structure matures and urbanization process progresses, the relative size of the middle class becomes bulged. However, poverty and inequality in income distribution inhibits the middle class from forming as a significant group.

In other areas of market deficiency, phenomenon such as the creation of new markets and the separation of old existing markets cannot be dealt with simply within the theory of market mechanism. These occurrences have been widely observed at times of social turmoil, like natural disasters or major social changes, or during times of huge technological changes.

Of course, it is well known that monopoly and oligopoly, when they exist, prohibit the achievement of competitive result of efficiency. These are known as market failure. That is why a system of anti-trust laws and regulation of mergers and acquisition is called for. However, it has been observed that oftentimes those regulations and legislations have been bent and obstructed by the political powers in favor of large enterprises and capitals.

Local currency movements were proposed to tackle with those problems of the modern monetary economy, in particular, with concerns of environmental issues and the need for revitalization of local small businesses (Hirst 1994).

7.3 Definition and Nature of Local Currency

Local currency is defined as a currency or a system of currency in which participants in certain regions or communities voluntarily exchange goods and services. The system of local currency is considered as an extension/development from the gift economy or the reciprocity economy. The early ideas of various forms of local currency for the purpose of supplementing the deficiency of national currency were brought about in 1930s, the time of the Great Depression (Keynes 1936). Recently, it survived again and was popularized in the 1980s mainly in Europe and the North America.

One of the pioneering systems, Local Exchange and Trading System (LETS) started in 1983 in Vancouver Island, Canada (http://www.transaction.net/

money/lets). There are number of other well-known local currencies, such as IthacaHours of Ithaca (http://www.ithacahours.org), New York, and Local Time Bank of Rome, Italy (http://www.timebanks.org).

In Japan, a large number of systems of local currencies were designed, practiced, and experimented. It is said that there were at one time more than 400 such systems or groups used local currencies in Japan in the early 2000s. One local currency, Kurin by Kuriyama-cho, Hokkaido is famous and has been active for long time. Another is Peanuts, of Chiba-city, Chiba, by which a group of shops along a street gathered and created the local currency.

The purposes of local currency have often been pursued for the followings:

(1) to seek to promote active transactions of goods and services based upon mutual trust and help, not on inhuman exchange for money only,
(2) to stimulate the growth of local economies by controlling prices locally and securing local employment,
(3) to activate transactions of goods and services according to the true needs of the local people, not for the accumulation of wealth, nor special interests and speculation,
(4) to provide social welfare, care for the aged, protection for the weak, the sick, and those who need help, and those services that are not easily provided by markets,
(5) to help promote and combine NPOs and NGOs which are working for social problems such as the environment, work conditions, welfare, poverty, and school systems by becoming a hub of the network of these organizations,
(6) to provide a basis and platform for the local people and community by making them aware of the possibilities of living diverse and rich lives without relying on money.

Any community that wants it to start a system of local currency can do so at its own will. Generally, there are only a few common features observed from experience and experiments. A civil group needs to start to organize. It is important to take note that it must truly be a civil and voluntary group that starts and manages the system, not some part of government, or in any sense a forced system. The effort and cost of management must be shared properly within the group. It must make sure that it does not place a burden on any particular part of the community. The area or region in which the system is maintained has to be relatively small and clearly defined. Usually the local currency is defined as non-convertible with the national money. There is no interest attached, sometimes there is time limit for the circulation, or its value may be decreased by a certain rate.

Thus, in general, local currency can be said that it is a "warm" money that people can make by their own will, the circulation of which is limited to a certain region, area, shops or people, and not to be used for the accumulation of wealth. It is strongly based on the local people's sense of trust and empathy. Local currency is not only a means of transaction for a local economy but also a means of bonding for the solidarity of the people.

In the next section, we take up the case of Yamaguchi Yapee which serves as an example of an experiment with the local currency that was practiced in Yamaguchi during 2000–2002.

7.4 An Example: Yamaguchi Yapee

Yamaguchi local currency, "Yapee" (pronounced as wha-pea), is a free money which makes people within the local region connect with each other based on trust and goodwill (Yamaguchi Local Currency Study Group 2010). Yapees can be earned by providing services that one is good at or goods that are no longer needed at home to those who may still need them. These Yapees can be used to exchange services that one is not good at doing or goods that are in need from those who have surpluses of those goods.

7.4.1 Yamaguchi Local Currency 'Yapee'

A local currency, Yapee, was created and experimented with twice during the period between April 2000 and March 2002 in Yamaguchi, Japan. The first round of transactions was carried out in-between April 2000 and March 2001. The second round was conducted in the period of April 2001 to March 2002.

The first round of experiments was organized by Yamaguchi Future-Time Bank (YFTB), a student-initiated volunteer activity group based at Yamaguchi Prefectural University, Yamaguchi City. The basic premises underlying YFTB's activities were the followings:

(1) Everyone, any one person, has something to offer to others; something s/he is good at, a special skill, or commendable feature, or seen as having a fantastic nature to others.
(2) It is not the amount of money but the quality of time that determines the quality of our lives, and ultimately, the degree of happiness (QOL).
(3) "We only have what we give. Things we want most in life are most easily attained by giving them to others." as Isabel Allende said.
(4) One hour of all the people must be worth equal to one hour of others.

It is interesting to note in relation to the third premise above that Pachacuti, a King of the Inca Empire, once said that we become richer by giving not by taking.

The naming of Future-Time Bank was the expression of the students' hope to make their future better than ever by promoting volunteer activities and to disseminate the idea of exchanging people's time and services in the form of deposit and future use just like Time-Dollar. The organizing group of students have tried to embody the above premises in their activities and enjoyed the close contacts and communication with local citizens, young and old.

On the other hand, the second round was organized and executed by the Yamaguchi Local Currency Research Committee for a much wider range of participants and variety of types of services and activities. More than one hundred and fifty people were involved and registered, including citizens, families, students, school administrators, teachers, civil servants, and business persons in the area. The majority of the people were from Yamaguchi City, but others from Hagi, Onoda, Shimonoseki and Hofu cities were also involved.

The major purposes of the first Yapee experiment were to promote community volunteer activities by the members, to exchange services and activities among people with more skills for something with those lesser means, and thus to contribute to higher awareness about the role of local currency in Yamaguchi community. Students have engaged in such volunteer activities as walking dogs and running errands for elderly people, teaching English at local elementary schools, helping children at hospitals, weeding the gardens, and baby-sitting. They earned 1 Yapee for 30 min of activities. Some students accumulate Yapees from hours of various activities and use them to get help from other members.

Having basically the same purposes as the first round, the second round intended to introduce the demurage, i.e., a negative interest rate or explicit statement of time limit for existence or use of Yapee. People had to use Yapee no matter how much accumulated definitely by a preset date of expiration of the local currency, Yapee. After the date of expiration, all and every remaining amount of Yapee was to become invalid. In other words, the local currency has a date of disappearance from the people.

With 6 months preparation for the transaction experiment of Yapee, the experiment had started on Sunday, November 11, 2001 by making that date the day of the first transaction and the event of Yapee Auction Game. More than 60 people participated in the Auction Game. Examples of goods and services provided for the auction were (1) a set of two dozen cans of soft drinks, (2) a coupon booklet for a restaurant, (3) 10 h of computer lessons (for a minimum of 10,000 Yapee), and (4) 6 h of English conversation lessons, among others. There were 21 items all together, and all were auctioned out on the day. This Auction Game was very successful in that not only were all the items sold out but that the event was carried out in the form of an auction game that gave the participants of the day better and deeper understanding about the nature and use of local currency.

In order to promote the transaction of goods and services available and in need from among the participants, a book that showed all the participants and each registered members' list of goods and services was made available to the members. There were around 100 individuals and 2 dozen business enterprises registered as members in this Yapee Transaction Game for about 7 weeks. The registered members were supposed to make contact with the other sides of the deals by checking the book and negotiate the Yapee price and other terms of conditions, such as date and place of transaction. Each and every transaction was required to be recorded into a postcard size card with columns for date, Yapee amount (either plus or minus), and names of the other sides of the transactions. It was just like a page of a saving book of a bank account, only one page the size of 10.5 cm in width and 14.8 cm in height. Extra cards were provided to those who needed them to record transactions beyond the eleven rows on one card can provide.

7.4.2 Results and Analysis of Yapee Experiment

At the end of the period of the Yapee Experiment, all the data of voluntary transactions through Yapee were collected. From this documentation, the information gathered the types of data that was used to analyze the entire range of people's activities including the kinds of transactions, the frequency of the transactions, the prices people agreed to attach to each deal, and the total number of members engaged in the Yapee transactions.

As seen in Tables 7.1 through 7.3, the number of members who actually have participated in this program was about one-third out of the total number registered which was approximately one hundred and thirty.

Table 7.1 shows that out of 47 people who returned their Yapee books, the two-third, 31 people engaged in actual transactions. The total number of transactions was 120, as can be seen from Table 7.3. The percentage of people who did not engage in any transaction was 34 %, which was about one-third of the people who had returned their reports. One transaction was carried out by 19 % of the people, two transactions by 8.5 %, and three transactions by 10.6 %. The fact that the percentage of people who had done five and six transactions were

Table 7.1 Transactions per person

# Transaction	# Persons	Percentage (%)
0	16	34.04
1	9	19.15
2	4	8.51
3	5	10.64
4	2	4.26
5	4	8.51
6	3	6.38
7	1	2.13
8	0	0
9	0	0
10	0	0
11	1	2.13
12	1	2.13
13	1	2.13
Total	47	

Average number of transaction per person = 2.55
Source YLCSG (2002)

Table 7.2 Balance per person

Balance	# of Person	Percentage (%)
~−10,000	1	2.13
~−5,000	1	2.13
~−4,000	1	2.13
~−3,000	2	4.26
~−2,000	0	0
~−1,000	7	14.89
0	18	38.30
~1,000	6	12.77
~2,000	1	2.13
~3,000	2	4.26
~4,000	0	0
~5,000	3	6.38
~6,000	0	0
~7,000	0	0
~8,000	2	4.26
~9,000	1	2.16
9,001~	2	4.26
Total	47	

Includes persons with no transaction
Source YLCSG (2002)

8.5 and 6.4 % shows that there was a significant number of people who were very active and who had engaged in activities. It is significant that there were people who did engage in 11, 12 and 13 transactions in numbers. The average number of transaction per person was 2.55, while the average transactions within those who had done any transaction (excluding no transaction) was 3.90. This means that the average number of transaction among those who had done any activity was about 4.

Table 7.2 shows the final balance of Yapees from reported cards out of about 7 weeks of activities. It shows that the category of people with zero final balance was the highest percentage. In this category, there was no distinction between no transaction and a zero final balance that involved transactions. The percentage of people with negative balances was 25.5 % and those with positive total balances was 36.2 %. From this data, we can say that (1) the percentage of people who did no transaction was the highest, (2) there were more people with positive balances than negative balances, and (3) the distribution of number of people with negative balances were gradually decreased as the amount increased, while those with positive balances had two peaks in the distribution.

Table 7.3 shows the distribution of the amount of Yapee per transaction. The highest category has transactions with more than 1,000 Yapee to below 2,000, which was 30.8 %. The next largest amount of Yapee transaction

Table 7.3 Yapee value per transaction

Yapee	# of Transaction	Percentage (%)
~1,000	30	25.00
~2,000	37	30.83
~3,000	17	14.17
~4,000	6	5.00
~5,000	12	10.00
~6,000	7	5.83
~7,000	5	4.17
~8,000	4	3.33
Unknown	2	1.67
Total	120	

Source YLCSG (2002)

was 1,000 Yapee and less (25.0 %). The lowest three categories, under 3,000 Yapees per transaction, shared 70.0 % of the total. The next largest group of transactions had values of more than 4,000 and under 5,000 (10.0 %). The higher the value of transaction, the smaller is the percentage of transactions beyond 6,000 Yapee.

Some opinions and suggestions from the questionnaire returned from the participants are summarized and representative ones are listed below:

(1) It was an interesting project but I could not participate actively. If the project is repeated, I would like to participate actively.
(2) It was a very short time of period. Hoping to extend the time period longer next time.
(3) The idea of 'local currency' sounded very interesting but I could not understand well.
(4) The difficult part of the project of this game (experiment) was that I had to get contact those whom I do not know, and that I had to ask unknown people to do something.
(5) If there had been an office or managing people for matching buys and sells, it would have been much easier for people to engage in these transactions than the ones done in the Yapee game this time.
(6) Because I had a very busy schedule, I could not participate as much as I wanted.
(7) Because people were not familiar with the auction and the game of voluntary transactions, people needed more time to get used to it all.
(8) In order to have more business enterprises involvement, the aspects of regional revitalization, social contribution, and enhancing communication within the community should have been emphasized more. However, it was good that people from different backgrounds like university students, professors, families, citizens, business enterprises, and people of different generations had worked together for the local area's revitalization.

7.5 Factors for Success and Failure

There are numbers of things that we can learn from the past experiences of local currency practices and experiments in various parts of the world. Let us summarize some of the advantages and disadvantages of local money in order to see clearly the factors of successes and/or failures.

Advantages

1. Networking opportunity with people whom one may not have known otherwise.
2. It is possible that things and activities which are important to the particular region are exchanged. These important activities and commodities may not have been revealed with the market transaction only.
3. New community businesses may be born as a result of local currency circulation.
4. It may be a true joy to see that one's special talent or gift can be positively used to help others in a community directly.
5. Activities using a local currency may be complementary utilized to fill in the fields and areas in which public services may not be enough.
6. Local currency may be effective to revitalize local businesses or shops.
7. It is possible to participate in the offering and receiving of services and goods in the system of local currency without regard to people's ability and wealth.

Disadvantages

1. It may be difficult and not easily be achieved completing transactions of goods and services directly with strangers. A help of courage may be needed to actively participate in the circulation of local currency.
2. It may be cumbersome to record each and every transaction in the book, if paper money or some other token is not used.
3. People may be reluctant to exchange economically high-value activities as local currency transaction.
4. It may not be easy for some one to be asked to offer services in the community, while it is easy to offer services.
5. Insurance may be needed to assure the safety of people in the system of the local currency.
6. In order to promote exchange activity, for buying and selling, an office and coordinator of the system may be needed.
7. Administration in the office may be tedious and quite complicated.

Through the various experiments and actual experiences mentioned above in this chapter, the success or failure of the use of local currency actually depends on local conditions and the design of the system of local currency. It is one thing that the idea of local currency explained is generally welcomed by many people at first, but actual participation in a particular system is quite another thing to most of the people. In many places, even with heavy preparation of at least 6 months or longer and passionate persuasion the percentage of people who actively engage in exchange activities would be about 50 % out of the total number of registered. The time period of operation may be 3–6 months. If it is longer than that people may lose excitement and momentum, and the kinds and numbers of exchangeable goods and services would diminish rapidly.

There are some important factors for successful design of the local currency circulation that we can learn from past experiences. Let us mention some of these below;

- The role of a central office of administration is important in terms of promoting participation of people, coordination of activities, and assurance of true and genuine social experiment. Managers and coordinators can design the whole and entire mechanism including whether they use money or a book type for record depending upon local needs. Office staff can play multi-dimensional roles for the local currency system because the people may not be familiar with the new system.
- It may be helpful to clearly define the major purposes and rules concerning the types of goods and services, whether members include only individuals, or whether businesses and organizations may be included. Misunderstanding can often happen with regard to the rules, purposes, coverage of goods and services dealt, and time and places for transactions since people have different expectations for different individual purposes.
- There may not exist such a thing as optimum size of scale or number of participants. However, in order to have a large enough number of activities and different types, the minimum would be 100–150 people for registration. Even with that number of people registered, it is expected to have one-third of people inactive.
- Time limit may rejuvenate activities. With 3–4 month rest period, another circulation period of, say, 6 months would be good for members to have active, up-beat behavior in the system. Placing a terminal time limit for exchange may make people behave differently from having no time limit.
- Mutual help in daily life, repeatable services, and inter-generational exchange activities should be encouraged to put into the list of wants and/or can-do. This list of activities would be the first bases for people to entice active involvement. Variety and kinds of goods and services are expected to be plenty and in wide range.

7.6 Further Considerations

- Think up your favorite name for a local currency in your area, supposing that you are the manager of a new local currency experiment. Which form of money do you think the local people in your area would prefer, paper money, metal/plastic tips, paper accounts, or even digital money?
- Consider two or three purposes for the new mechanism of your local currency in the region.
- Consider one or two special features in order to make your local business, community and school systems interested in and actively participate in your experiment of a local currency.

References

Fisher I (1932) Booms and depressions: some first principles. Adelphi Company, New York
Hirst P (1994) Associate democracy: new forms of economic and social governance. Polity Press, Cambridge
Keynes JM (1936/2007) The general theory of employment, interest and money. Palgrave Macmillan, Basingstoke
Yamaguchi Local Currency Study Group (2002) Experiment/research report of Yamaguchi Local Currency Study Group 2002. Yamaguchi

Chapter 8
Role of Solidarity in Organic Agriculture

Ki-Hueng Kim and Yukio Ikemoto

Abstract In this chapter we see how organic agriculture depends on solidarity between farmers and consumers. The purposes of protecting environment and human health cannot be achieved without a healthy society in which people know the situation of each other and the impact of their conducts on the environment and their neighbors. On the other hand, modern technology such as chemical fertilizers and pesticides deprived us of our understanding of environment and society. Many people are now interested in organic agriculture but the basis is our concern for a healthy society and therefore solidarity. Organic agriculture is a holistic system which promotes and enhances ecosystem, health, food safety and local environment etc. Organic agriculture can be roughly divided into two types, maintaining face-to-face relationships and the certification type found in Japan. In Korea, these days market of certified products is becoming more and more competitive, so that farmers with less competitiveness turn towards direct relationships with local consumers. In the Northeastern Thailand, many groups are performing organic agriculture already and these days local government has been promoting the organic agriculture.

Keywords Organic agriculture · *Teikei* · Face to face relationship · Capability approach · Japan · Korea · Thailand

K.-H. Kim (✉)
Chungnam Development Institute, 73-26 Yeonsuwon-gil, Gongju-si,
Chungcheongnam-do, South Korea
e-mail: kihuengkim@gmail.com

Y. Ikemoto
Institute for Advanced Studies on Asia, The University of Tokyo, 7-3-1 Hongo,
Bunkyo-ku, Tokyo 113-0033, Japan

N. Matsui and Y. Ikemoto (eds.), *Solidarity Economy and Social Business*,
SpringerBriefs in Economics, DOI 10.1007/978-4-431-55471-4_8

8.1 Introduction

It is widely believed that organic agriculture is just a matter of farming technique which does not use chemical fertilizer and pesticides. However, this understanding is very narrow and neglects its impact on human society. What organic farmers are pursuing under the name of organic agriculture extends to the environment of the entire human society. According to International Federation of Organic Agriculture Movements, organic agriculture is a production system that sustains the health of soils, ecosystem and people. This means that it aims to be a holistic system which promotes ecosystem, human health, food safety, environment, etc. Non-usage of chemicals is just a condition to make our society and environment healthy in a broad sense, which is its ultimate goal. This indicates that chemicals damage not only nature and human health but also human society. If farmers do not care about health and environment of consumers, they may use a lot of chemicals in order to increase income, even though it may damage the environment and consumers' health. On the other hand, if consumers do not know how chemicals affect our health and environment and how their foods are produced, they will choose cheap and superficially nice vegetables, even though they may be harmful to the environment and health. In order to avoid such damages, farmers and consumers need to know each other and behave with a broader perspective.

If we hope to have a healthy society, we need a society that protects our health and environment. This means that a healthy society takes actions to avoid problems. Of course, a healthy society is not just a means but also our goal. Non-usage of chemicals is only a small part of the organic agriculture and a symbol for a movement to restore healthy society.

In this chapter, we focus on the relationship between agriculture and society. In order to make organic agriculture sustainable, a close relationship, or solidarity, between farmers and consumers is needed. They need to support each other. And they need to conduct many kinds of activities to know each other as we will see in this chapter. In the next section we will take up the Japanese case and explain how solidarity is important for organic agriculture. In Sects. 8.3 and 8.4 we will discuss the cases of Korea and Thailand.

8.2 *Teikei*: Organic Agriculture in Japan

Teikei is a key word for the organic agriculture movement in Japan. *Teikei* is a Japanese word which means cooperation, alliance, or association, and in the context of organic agriculture it means maintaining a close relationship between consumers and farmers. In the early 1970s when the environmental problems became more and more serious in Japan, consumers in urban areas who were very anxious about food safety met directly with farmers in rural areas who were concerned about their own health problems caused by the chemicals used for the modern agriculture and they agreed that the farmers produce organic products for the consumers and that the consumers buy the products. This was the beginning of organic agriculture in Japan. This shows that the problems they faced could not be solved just by the market mechanism and that they need direct cooperation to overcome the market failure (Kim 2011). We can find solidarity here and we will show that organic agriculture need solidarity.

The Japan Organic Agriculture Association was founded in 1971 to promote organic agriculture in Japan whose members includes both farmers and consumers. From the beginning it has been emphasizing *Teikei* between farmers and consumers as one of its basic principles. They needed to support each other and so mutual understanding was indispensable to make the relationship sustainable. They had many chances to meet each other. The farmers brought their products to the consumers by themselves and the consumers often visited the farmers to see how they were working. In other words, the market brought very limited information to each other. They are connected only by prices. Such a narrow informational base of the market mechanism was not enough for mutual understanding. In fact, there are many cases of organic agriculture in the world which depend on maintaining a close relationship such as Community Supported Agriculture (CSA) in the United States, AMAP (Associations pour le Maintien d'une Agriculture Paysanne; associations to sustain agriculture and farmers) in France, and ACP (Agriculture Contractuelle de Proximite; contract agriculture for local farmers and consumers) in Switzerland.

In the 1980s when organic agriculture became popular among Japanese people, non-organic products were sometimes sold as "organic" because they could be sold at a higher price. In order to cope with this kind of false labeling, the Japanese government began to consider introducing a standard for organic products. In 1992, the Ministry of Agriculture, Forestry and Fisheries of Japan established a guideline for labeling "organic." And in 1999, by revising Japanese Agricultural Standard (JAS), agricultural products can be labeled "organic" only when they were certified by a third-party organization (Honjo 2004; Kubota 2001). This certificate was very beneficial for large-scale producers who sell a large amount of their products to remote markets. For them, *Teikei* or face-to-face relationships were not necessary to sell their products. Certificates were enough for them. However, the certificate can convey very limited information on the farming technique. It does not convey any information about the environment and local society in the producing areas. On the other hand, consumers who are interested only in the quality of the food, not in the environment and rural society, are willing to buy the products. Even though the certificate can convey very limited information, it has an effect to connect farmers and consumers. It is a limited kind of solidarity.

While large-scale farmers took advantage of the certificate and succeeded in expanding their market, small-scale farmers gave up getting the certificate because they could not afford the expense of getting it. Very ironically, although they have been in the mainstream of the Japanese organic agriculture movement and practicing what Japanese organic agriculture pursued from the beginning, they had to give up using the word "organic" because their products are not certified.[1] They,

[1] It is interesting to note that the different strategies of the large-scale and small-scale farmers corresponds to the two solutions which Axelrod showed to overcome the market failure, that is, label and territoriality (Axelrod 1984). In the case of organic agriculture, label corresponds to the certificate while territoriality corresponds to Teikei and face-to-face relationships (Kim 2009).

on the contrary, depend more on face-to-face relationships. They re-emphasized and strengthened *Teikei* with their customers. They had to rely on *Teikei* to continue organic agriculture without the certificate. They needed consumers' understanding. They organized events for their customers to join agricultural activities such as planting rice seedlings, harvesting rice and potatoes, tea-picking, and so on. They also organized harvest festivals and cooking schools for their consumers. The consumers in urban areas sometimes do not know how to cook traditional vegetables and so the farmers teach them how to cook them. They also organize excursion for nature observation. Farmers think these activities are their duty and they find happiness in them. These activities are very useful for revitalizing the depopulated areas. They teach farming technique to those who want to start agriculture. Thus organic agriculture is following many roles from environmental protection to sustaining society.

Even though they may not earn a lot of money like the large-scale farms, they may not be as unhappy as we expect because their main purpose is not to earn money but to achieve better quality of life and to protect the environment. Therefore, it is not fair for them to evaluate their activities in terms of income. If we want to evaluate their activities in a more appropriate way, we need a broader informational base than income. Amartya Sen proposes to use his capability approach to evaluate human well-being.[2] His concept of capability is defined as a set of what a person can do and can be. Exactly speaking, it is "the alternative combination of functionings that are feasible for her to achieve. Capability is thus a kind of freedom" (Sen 1999, p. 75). The basic idea of the capability approach is that we can evaluate a person's well-being by what he/she can do and can be. To be healthy is, of course, an important functioning for human well-being. The capability ranges from the basic one such as "being healthy" and "being adequately nourished" to a more complex one such as "being happy," "having self-respect," and "taking part in the life of community" (Sen 1992, p. 39).

These complex functionings are also important for organic farmers. For example, their activities known as *Teikei* are to take part in the life of community. They are satisfied with organic farming and they have self-respect in contributing to society and environmental protection. Though Sen does not show what should be included in the capability, Martha Nussbaum who developed the concept with Sen gave a list of functionings that we should focus on. One of the functionings in the list is affiliation, which is "Being able to live with and toward others, to recognize and show concern for other human beings, to engage in various forms of social interaction; to be able to imagine the situation of another and to have compassion for that situation; to have the capability for both justice and friendship. (Protecting this capability means protecting institutions that constitute and nourish such forms of affiliation, and also protecting the freedom of assembly and political speech.)" (Nussbaum 2000). It is very clear that *Teikei* is a kind of affiliation and is an important part of human well-being. Thus *Teikei* is not only a means

[2] The capability approach can be used for evaluating human development, inequality and poverty, too.

for establishing organic agriculture but also an end for human life. Nussbaum also listed other functionings such as environment and play. From the viewpoint of Nussbaum's capability list, organic farmers may be achieving much higher capability than other people (Ikemoto and Kim 2008).

8.3 Environment-Friendly Agriculture in Korea

In Korea, organic agriculture began in the mid-1970s with the efforts of conscious farmers and civil groups as was the case in Japan. 'Jeong-nong,' one of the major organic agricultural groups in Korea, was established in 1976, focusing on protecting the environment and revitalizing local communities. In this period, the market for organic products was very limited and the farmers had to sell their products directly to the civil groups. In the 1980s as the organic agriculture expanded, the farmers began to sell their products on the market.

The 1990s was a turning point for Korea as well as for the world (Huh 2000). In 1992, the United Nations Conference on Environment and Development (UNCED), the so-called Earth Summit, was held in Rio de Janeiro and Agenda 21 was adopted. In Korea, phenol outflowed from a factory into Rakdong River in March 1991, which made people much more environment-conscious. This incident reflected the poor ethics of Korean society for environment in those days when the Korean economy achieved a high growth rate and 'polluting industries' pursued economic growth at the cost of environment. Similarly the agricultural policy aimed mainly to increase food production using a lot of chemical fertilizer and pesticides, neglecting their impact on environment. The policies were oriented toward income generation, efficiency and large-scale farming.

However, after this incident, Korean people become more conscious about environmental problems and a full-scale civic movement and environmental movement followed. Consumers became more conscious about food safety and were willing to pay more for safe foods. With the rising consciousness of the people, the Korean government began to promote organic farming under the name of "environment-friendly agriculture" with the enactment of *the Environment-friendly Agriculture Promotion Act* in 1997. And the year 1998 was declared as the starting year of environment-friendly agriculture. Several concrete support actions were initiated in 1999 such as 'Support for Building a Sustainable Agriculture Zone,' 'Pilot Villages for Environment-friendly Agriculture,' and 'Direct Payment for Environment-friendly Agriculture' (Heo 2000). Environment-friendly agriculture is defined as a farming technique to increase farm household income while pursuing both environmental preservation and safety of agricultural products to induce sustainable agricultural production by harmonizing agriculture with environment (Ministry of Agriculture, Food and Rural Affairs, Korea, 1997).

The leadership of the Minister of Agriculture, Food and Rural Affairs played a prominent role in changing the agricultural policy from conventional agriculture to environment-friendly agriculture. In fact, at the beginning, most of the government officials and researchers in the Ministry expressed a skeptical view of the new policy. However, with the leadership of the Minister, they gradually changed their view and began to approve it after the law was enacted (Adachi 2002).

These policies successfully increased environment-friendly agriculture rapidly. Most of the farmers turned to more environmentally friendly agriculture. In this transition, the certificates of environment-friendly agriculture played an important role because farmers could get various kinds of supports from the government if they got the certificates. So farmers were eager to get the certificates. Recently, less competitive organic groups are now turning to the direct sale to local consumers as is the case of *Teikei* in Japan. 'Paldang Sengmyung Salim' group which was strongly influenced by 'Jeong-nong' also sold their products to the market through the Agricultural Cooperative after 2003 and they could make profits. However, as the market of the certified products became more and more competitive, they gradually lost the market. And finally they shifted to the direct sale to local consumers and local schools for student' lunch in 2007. At last they returned to their original purposes, namely to protect the environment revitalize local communities, and strengthened the ties or solidarity with local communities.

8.4 Sufficiency Economy in Thailand

King Rama IX of Thailand has been actively promoting the sufficiency economy. During the economic crisis in 1997, he criticized the income-oriented growth policies, which, he insisted, made the Thai economy vulnerable to external shocks and brought it into crisis. He insisted on depending on themselves instead of the external market to stabilize the economy. This means that farmers need to depend less on chemicals and to diversify their products to include not only rice but also vegetables, fruits, fishery, poultry and livestock. This is a recycling-oriented agriculture. Thus his idea is very close to the organic agriculture. His idea is also very close to Buddhism and his idea was accepted by many devout Buddhists and Buddhist monks spread his idea to the general public. In order to spread his idea, a lot of projects were conducted as Royal projects across the country and local governments also supported and promoted organic farming.

In Thailand there are many small groups of farmers which aim to establish a sufficiency economy. Some groups are established voluntarily, some are supported by local government, and some are recommended by Buddhist monks. For example, in Kalasin province of the northeast Thailand, which is known as the poorest region in Thailand, we met a famous Buddhist monk who supported villagers to establish agricultural cooperative in the early 2000s in order to support poor farmers. Many villagers responded and tried to realize his idea. In Thailand, villagers' mobility is very high and they have a network in rural areas. Through this network, the monks' idea spread widely and many farmers groups were established in the northeast region. They not only spread the idea but also the know-how to manage the sufficiency economy. Thus solidarity within the farmers groups is spreading through this network to other groups.

Provincial and district governments also supported the establishment of farmer groups and held training courses for farmers, conducted at model farms or successful cases. For example, Kalasin provincial government has been supporting farmers groups since 2007. To support the organic farmers, many kinds of programs are implemented such as farmers' schools for group leaders, demonstration of how to make organic fertilizer for farmers, and sales of organic products at exhibitions in urban areas.

Organic products are often faced with the problem of marketing. They need a market where their products can be sold at higher prices. Each group is doing its best to find out its own market. For example, in the case of Kalasin province mentioned above, the monk succeeded in establishing a rice mill as a Royal project. This rice mill buys organic rice directly from farmers with a premium at a higher price than the traditional rice which uses chemicals. Since they don't need to sell to middlemen, they can earn more. The rice which was milled at this factory was send to Bangkok and sold at the temples with which the monk has a close relationship. The transaction of rice is managed by volunteer groups of the temples. They often visit the Royal rice mill and villages to help poor people. And so they know the situation in rural areas very well. When they sell the rice, they use a logo of the Royal project and explain the background of the rice. Since the people who visit the temples have religious orientations to help poor people and also knowledge that organic products are good for health, they are willing to pay more for the rice. Therefore the volunteer groups can sell the rice to people at a higher price than the market by explaining the situation of the farmers and how good it is for health. Though the consumers in urban areas don't meet the farmers directly, they can feel solidarity with the farmers. What is needed to make organic agriculture sustainable is a mechanism to connect consumers with the farmers or solidarity between them. Here we can see solidarity between consumers and farmers with the efforts of the intermediary volunteer groups.

In Thailand, the regional income gap between Bangkok, the primate capital city of Thailand, and other regions, especially the northeast region, is very high and it became a factor of the current political conflict in Thailand. The country seems to be divided into the "rich" Bangkok and the "poor" northeast which are in conflict with each other. Even though the conflict among politicians is still fierce, general people began to learn the situation of each other and feel solidarity as the case mentioned above. We need to make steady efforts to establish solidarity in the country and organic agriculture is taking a role for this purpose.

8.5 Further Considerations

- Consider how to make face-to-face relationships for new farmers' groups.
- Consider support programs for organic agriculture.

References

Adachi K (2002) Korean agricultural policies shift towards an environmentally friendly agriculture: an interview with Minister of Agriculture and Chief of Staff of Agriculture in the Executive Mansion. J Agric Policy Res 2:220–232 (in Japanese)
Axelrod R (1984) The evolution of cooperation. Basic Books Inc., Publishers, New York
Heo J (2000) An empirical assessment of environment-friendly agriculture programs. Korea Rural Econ Rev 23(1) (Korea Rural Economic Institute, in Korean)
Honjo N (2004) Organic agriculture in Japan-problem of policies and institution. Noubunkyo (in Japanese)
Huh G-H (2000) Emerging issues for Korean agriculture in the 21st century. Korea Rural Econ Rev 23(1) (Korea Rural Economic Institute, in Korean)
Ikemoto Y, Kim K-H (2008) Organic Farming and Amartya Sen's capability approach. Kokugakuin Univ Econ Rev 56(3, 4):437–481 (Kokugakuin University, in Japanese)
Kim K-H (2009) The role and challenges of organic agriculture: comparative study between Japan and Korea. Doctoral degree, The University of Tokyo (In Japanese)
Kim K-H (2011) Local-based organic agriculture: experience of Japan and Korea. Tsukuba-shobo, Japan (In Japanese)
Kubota H (2001) Perspective of organic agriculture movement and JAS of organic agricultural products. Kokugakuin Econ No 49-1 (In Japanese)
Nussbaum MC (2000) Women and human development: the capabilities approach. Cambridge University Press, Cambridge
Sen AK (1992) Inequality examined. Harvard University Press, Cambridge
Sen AK (1999) Development as freedom. Knopf Press, New York

Chapter 9
Certified Coffee and Solidarity

Yukio Ikemoto

Abstract During the Coffee Crisis in the early 2000s, consumers in developed countries enjoyed cheap coffee while coffee farmers in developing countries suffered from poverty. Thus globalization disconnected the farmers in developing countries and consumers in developed countries. Farmers are interested only to increase the production volume and they do not care for what kind of coffee the consumers may prefer. On the other hand, the consumers are looking for cheap coffee products and do not care the impacts of their behavior on the environment and the life of the farmers. After the Coffee Crisis, consumers began to know this relationship and some of them tried to help the poor farmers by buying at higher price as is the case of Fair Trade. In the same way, some of them who are interested in environmental protection and willing to pay more to avoid environmental destruction supported other certified coffee such as Rainforest Alliance. It is not easy for consumers to contact directly with farmers and we need intermediaries to connect them. In the case of coffee this role is taken by the certificates such as Fair Trade. Even though the percentage of certified coffee may be small, its influence is widespread. With the development of information technology, the role of such intermediaries will be more and more important.

Keywords Coffee · Coffee crisis · Fair trade · Poverty alleviation · Vietnam · Certification · Coffee farmers

9.1 Introduction

It was in the 1990s that coffee production in the world increased dramatically, partly due to the efforts of the farmers, governments, international organizations, and both domestic and international NGOs for poverty alleviation and partly due

Y. Ikemoto (✉)
Institute for Advanced Studies on Asia, The University of Tokyo, 7-3-1 Hongo,
Bunkyo-ku, Tokyo 113-0033, Japan
e-mail: ikemoto@ioc.u-tokyo.ac.jp

N. Matsui and Y. Ikemoto (eds.), *Solidarity Economy and Social Business*,
SpringerBriefs in Economics, DOI 10.1007/978-4-431-55471-4_9

to the coffee boom in the mid-1990s in the world market. During this period, the focus of international development aid shifted from economic growth to poverty alleviation (World Bank 2001) and much attention was paid to coffee because it was considered suitable for poverty alleviation in the tropical mountainous areas. Coffee is one of the few commercial agricultural products that can be grown in mountainous areas in the tropics. Coffee cultivation is also environment-friendly if coffee trees are grown appropriately under shade trees. However, it was very ironic that the efforts to alleviate poverty resulted in the so-called Coffee Crisis in which the world coffee price dropped to a historically low level in the early 2000s so that many coffee farmers in many developing countries fell into serious poverty (Gresser and Tickell 2002). Especially those farmers who had just started growing coffee in the midst of the coffee boom by borrowing money to buy land and inputs for growing coffee and could harvest only after the price fall suffered seriously. They had no profit to repay the borrowed money.

Brazil and Vietnam are the two countries that increased coffee export very rapidly in the late 1990s.[1] It is well known that Brazil has been the largest coffee producing and exporting country in the world for many years. On the other hand, Vietnam, the second largest coffee exporting country in the world, is a new comer, which was only a minor coffee exporting country in the early 1990s. The growth of Vietnamese coffee export was so impressive that Vietnam has often been blamed for causing the Coffee Crisis. The argument was very simple that the rapidly increasing Vietnamese coffee export brought about oversupply in the world market, which led to the collapse of the world coffee price (Ikemoto and H'wen 2003). However, Vietnam was just following the rules of market mechanism. Vietnam was very successful. It is not Vietnam but the market mechanism that should be blamed for causing the Coffee Crisis. The market mechanism is often believed to be a panacea for economic problems but defects of the market mechanism are also well known. The cyclical fluctuation of agricultural price and products, which is applicable to the case of Coffee Crisis, is known as the cobweb theorem in the textbook of microeconomics.

A defect of the global market is the fact that the producers and consumers are detached from each other. Farmers are trying to produce as much as possible to earn more income irrespective of quality. They do not care about what consumers want. On the other hand, consumers are seeking cheap products and do not mind the poverty of coffee farmers and the environmental impact of coffee cultivation. Farmers and consumers are connected only by the price. A way to solve the problems of the global market is to connect producers and consumers in some way. And this means the solidarity between them at the global level. Many activities have already been created to solve this problem and other problems of poverty and environment. Fair trade is one of them. The certificates and labels take the role of connecting people. Many other activities and certificates became popular during and after the Coffee Crisis. The problems that were caused by losing relationships within globalization can and should be solved by restoring relationships.

---

[1] See Phan et al. (2007) for more detailed analysis on the relationship between Vietnamese coffee and ethnic minority people.

The organization of this chapter is as follows: Sect. 9.2 explains the basic characteristics of coffee cultivation, how they are related to environment and poverty alleviation policies, and how the Coffee Crisis occurred in the early 2000s. Section 9.3 argues how Vietnam succeeded in increasing coffee export and how the Coffee Crisis was related to globalization which has disconnected the farmers in developing countries and the consumers in developed countries. Section 9.4 argues solidarity as a means to solve problem such as poverty and environmental destruction by connecting the farmers with the consumers.

9.2 Coffee, Environment, and Poverty Alleviation

Major coffee producing areas spread along the so-called "coffee belt," which lies in the intertropical areas around the world. Within this coffee belt, the areas that actually meet the conditions for growing coffee are limited to the mountainous areas whose altitude is more than 1,000 m above sea level where the average annual temperature is between 18 and 25 °C and the average annual rainfall is more than 1,600 mm.[2] The reason why the coffee growing areas are very limited is that coffee trees are easily damaged by diseases and abnormal weather such as frost and drought. For example, at lower altitudes where the temperature is higher, coffee trees are affected adversely by the heat while on the other hand, at higher altitudes where the temperature is lower, coffee trees are damaged by frost. This fact of nature sometimes causes a very big periodic fluctuation of world coffee price. The world coffee price is heavily affected by the production of Brazil, the largest coffee producing country in the world. Brazilian coffee has been affected nearly once a decade by frost and drought since the 1970s, which made world coffee prices fluctuate violently (Fig. 9.1). The coffee price increases in the mid-1970s and mid-1990s were caused by the crop failures by frost in Brazil and those in the mid-1980s was caused by the crop failure by drought in Brazil. Since Brazil accounts for about 30 % in the world coffee production, its crop failure brought about a serious shortage in the world coffee market and therefore increased world coffee prices. In this sense, coffee is a very risky commodity and its volatility characterizes the international coffee market, which brings about sometimes windfall profits and sometimes tragedy. And this is also a reason for speculative money flows into the world coffee market from time to time.

Coffee trees are also damaged by disease and insects very seriously. In the history of coffee, the most serious damage was caused by the rust disease that destroyed Sri Lankan coffee completely in the late 19th century. In those days Sri Lanka was a major coffee exporting country but because of the damage, Sri Lanka abandoned coffee growing and shifted to tea growing, and it is now popular as the world's major tea exporting country. Among the other major coffee exporting countries, Indonesia

[2] This is the case for Arabica coffee. The other species of coffee such as Robusta can be grown at lower altitude and higher temperature. The difference between Arabica and Robusta will be explained in Sect. 9.3 of this chapter.

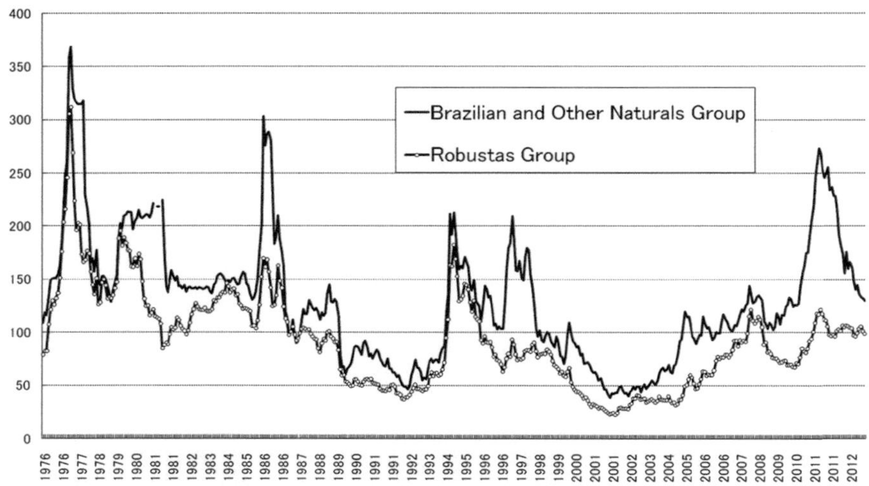

Fig. 9.1 World coffee prices index, 1976–2012. *Source* Drawn using the historical data in the website of International Coffee Organization

was also affected by the rust disease but did not give up growing coffee. It continued growing coffee by shifting to Robusta, another species of coffee, which, as the name indicates, is much stronger than Arabica to heat and disease.

The natural conditions for growing coffee are closely related to the recent concerns of the international community, namely deforestation and poverty. Since coffee trees are planted in the mountainous areas, new forests may be opened up to grow coffee, which may result in deforestation in some cases. However, coffee cultivation can contribute to biodiversity if coffee trees are grown under shade trees. As mentioned above, coffee, especially Arabica, is not strong against the heat and needed to be planted not only in the mountainous areas but also covered with shade trees. Shade trees are intercropped between coffee trees to cover coffee trees with their leaves to protect them from the strong tropical sunlight. Various kinds of trees can be used as shade trees, and this contributes to biodiversity. In this sense, coffee grown in this way is considered environment-friendly, which is the reason why shade trees are recommended by some NGOs.[3]

On the other hand, coffee cultivation has been introduced as a measure to alleviate poverty in the mountainous areas in the world. The people living in the mountainous areas who are often ethnic minority people are considered poor, depending on shifting cultivation. For them, coffee is one of the important and promising cash crops to increase income. It is also considered desirable to stop shifting cultivation, which is often accused of causing deforestation. This is one of the reasons why the supply of coffee in the world market grew in the late 1990s and the early 2000s.

[3] The effectiveness of the shade tree in reducing risks economically and environmentally is advocated by some organizations. See http://nationalzoo.si.edu/scbi/migratorybirds/coffee/lover.cfm.

Another reason for increasing supply of coffee was the market mechanism. The price hike in the mid-1990s as mentioned above brought about windfall gains for many farmers in the world except Brazil if their harvest was not damaged. The windfall gains became a stimulus for the existing coffee farmers to expand coffee growing and for newcomers to begin coffee growing. According to this market signal, many farmers began to expand coffee growing. However, the high prices continued only for a few years. When coffee production was recovered in Brazil, the coffee price lowered to the normal level. What is worse, coffee supply in the world market was increased because of expansion of coffee growing in other countries, which resulted in the oversupply of coffee in the world market. This eventually pulled the world prices down lower than before. Coffee farmers could not gain the profits as they expected. The situation was much more difficult for the newcomers who just started growing coffee after the coffee price increase and could not harvest before the price fall. Since it takes 3–4 years for coffee trees to bear fruits, if farmers start growing coffee in the midst of coffee boom, the price will be down when they begin to harvest.[4]

It is interesting to mention that the world coffee price increase in 1997 was not caused by crop failure in Brazil or in any other countries. It is said that it was caused by the speculative money of hedge funds and other commodity funds flowing into the world coffee market. Just a few months after the coffee price reached to the peak in May 1997, Thailand was forced to abandon its foreign exchange policy by the speculative attack of hedge funds, from which the financial crisis spread to other East and Southeast Asian countries.

After that, coffee price began to decrease very rapidly until 2002 to the 30-year low, which was called "Coffee Crisis."[5] It is very ironical that coffee growing was promoted to alleviate poverty but it resulted in worsening poverty among coffee farmers, not only the newcomers but also the long-experienced coffee farmers. It should be noticed that the oversupply of coffee benefitted those who buy the coffee at a cheaper price, not only the big companies of the coffee industries but also general consumers. In a sense, the efforts for the sake of the poor people in developing countries resulted in benefiting the coffee industry and consumers in developed countries who enjoyed cheap coffee at the cost of poverty of farmers in developing countries. This situation is very unequal and cannot be ethically sustainable. Those who realized this unequal situation started activities to help the suffered coffee farmers. In a global perspective which includes not only farmers in developing countries and consumers in the developed countries but also all intermediaries between them, this unequal situation is not economically sustainable. In this unequal situation, coffee growers cannot expect enough profit to invest even for maintaining the quality of coffee and as a result the quality of coffee will deteriorate. If consumers know that the quality of coffee was deteriorating, they may stop drinking coffee and coffee consumption would decrease. In this way the coffee industry will not be sustainable.

---

[4] This phenomenon often appears in the case of agricultural products, which is known as the cobweb theorem in economics.

[5] This reminds us of the export pessimism of the Prebisch-Singer thesis.

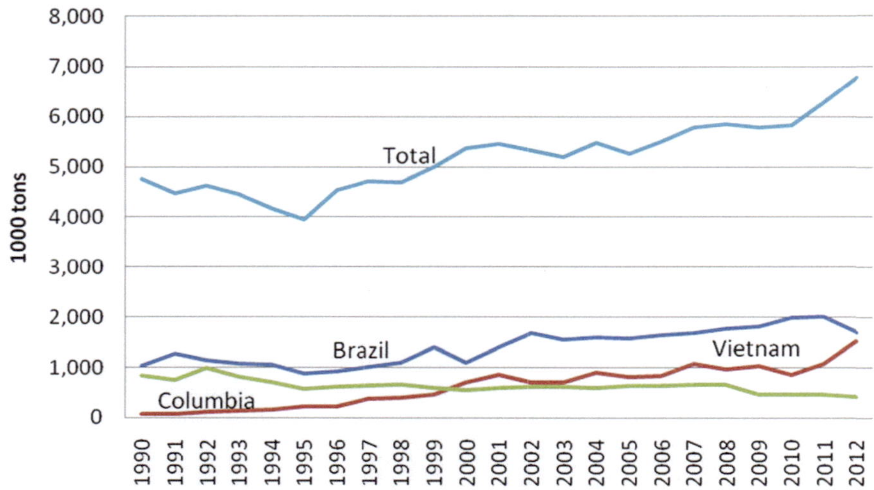

Fig. 9.2 World coffee export. *Source* Drawn by the author using the historical data in the website of International Coffee Organization

9.3 Coffee and Poverty in Vietnam

Vietnam was and still is often accused of causing the Coffee Crisis by oversupplying coffee in the world market. In fact, Vietnam increased its export as shown in Fig. 9.2 and Table 9.1. Vietnam was just a minor coffee exporting country in the early 1990s but succeeded in increasing coffee export to become the second largest coffee exporting country in the world at the end of the 1990s. This shows how rapidly Vietnam increased coffee export. However, we need to discuss some points before blaming Vietnam for causing the Coffee Crisis. One point is that Vietnam as a leading Robusta producing country was responsible for the oversupply in the Robusta market[6] but that it is not clear how it affected the Arabica market. And another point is that Vietnam was just following the rule of the market mechanism and proved its efficiency. In this perspective, it is not Vietnam but the market mechanism that should be blamed for the causes of the Coffee Crisis. And from this argument it follows that we need solidarity economy to overcome the problems caused by the market mechanism.

Before discussing the solidarity economy, it is interesting to discuss the first point, namely the relationship between Robusta and Arabica from the viewpoint of

6 "Available supplies of robusta were particularly high, but demand continued to concentrate more on arabicas. Increasing fierce competition in robusta was anticipated, given that large crops were also expected in Indonesia and India as well as in Vietnam. … In 2000, coffee prices fell to the depressed levels of 1992/1993 that preceded frosts in Brazil. The chief contributor to this was Vietnam, which has become the world's second biggest coffee producer, ahead of Colombia. … The most dramatic prices losses were for robusta—of which Vietnam is now the world's leading producer—with robusta prices hitting their lowest level since 1975" (UNCTD and CyclOple 2000, p. 173).

Table 9.1 Share of the world coffee export: 1990–2012

	Brazil	Vietnam	Columbia	Others	Total
1990	21.4	1.4	17.6	59.6	100.0
1991	28.4	1.6	16.9	53.1	100.0
1992	24.4	2.5	21.5	51.6	100.0
1993	24.1	2.8	18.3	54.8	100.0
1994	24.9	3.9	17.0	54.2	100.0
1995	22.0	5.4	14.9	57.7	100.0
1996	20.1	5.0	14.0	60.9	100.0
1997	21.4	7.9	13.9	56.8	100.0
1998	23.2	8.3	14.4	54.0	100.0
1999	27.8	9.3	12.0	51.0	100.0
2000	20.1	13.0	10.2	56.7	100.0
2001	25.5	15.5	10.9	48.0	100.0
2002	31.5	13.3	11.6	43.7	100.0
2003	29.8	13.5	11.9	44.9	100.0
2004	29.1	16.3	11.2	43.4	100.0
2005	29.9	15.3	12.4	42.3	100.0
2006	29.9	15.2	11.9	43.0	100.0
2007	29.3	18.6	11.7	40.4	100.0
2008	30.2	16.5	11.4	41.9	100.0
2009	31.5	17.7	8.2	42.5	100.0
2010	34.1	14.7	8.1	43.2	100.0
2011	32.0	16.9	7.4	43.7	100.0
2012	25.0	22.5	6.3	46.1	100.0

Source Calculated from the historical data in the website of International Coffee Organization

market mechanism. There are mainly two species of coffee, namely Arabica and Robusta.[7] And the species of coffee that Vietnam is mainly producing is Robusta. Arabica was the one that spreads to all around the world along the coffee belt for the first time in history. Arabica is of better quality than Robusta and therefore is more popular, accounting for three fourths of the world production. Taste is more important and differentiated by the name of the producing countries or localities. Usually consumers choose coffee by the name of the producing countries, localities or other brand names such as Blue Mountain. This situation of brand names matters only for Arabica, not for Robusta, which is the reason why the name of Vietnam is seldom heard as a coffee exporting country even though its share is the second largest in the world. Since Arabica is differentiated by the quality, the producers of Arabica coffee are very careful to maintain the high quality of coffee to keep the value of the brand name, which may keep its price high.

[7] Technically speaking, Robusta should be called *canephora*. However, Robusta is more popular and therefore Robusta is used in this chapter.

However, as mentioned above, Arabica is vulnerable and easily damaged by abnormal weather and diseases. This is the reason why coffee is grown in high-altitude mountainous areas. And this is the reason why Arabica is more expensive than Robusta. As the name indicates, Robusta is stronger and less affected by disease than Arabica so it can be grown in the low-altitude areas where Arabica cannot be grown or damaged by abnormal weather. In Vietnam, the area which is suitable geographically for growing Arabica is very limited and therefore almost all coffee growing areas are specialized to Robusta. The main coffee growing area is the Central Highlands near Cambodian and Laotian borders where the altitude is about 500–700 m from sea level. Robusta is so strong that it can be grown without shade trees, which means that Robusta-growing areas may be less biodiversified than Arabica-growing areas. To the contrary, shade trees are often undesirable for farmers from the economic viewpoint because more coffee trees can be grown without shade trees. The after-harvest processing method of Robusta, namely the so-called dry method, is much simpler than that of Arabica, which is called the wet method. In Vietnam, farmers dry the harvested coffee cherry[8] in the sun by themselves.

In spite of its strength and easiness, Robusta cannot replace Arabica completely because the taste of Robusta is widely considered inferior to Arabica. While Arabica is used for regular coffee, Robusta is mainly used for producing instant coffee (or soluble coffee). Since it is only an ingredient of instant coffee, the names of Robusta-producing countries seldom appear in the country-of-origin label of the products, which is the direct reason why Vietnam is not well known as major coffee exporting country. Since the name of the producing country does not appear for the case of Robusta, producers are much less interested in improving quality, which is contrary to the case of Arabica. This means that the information concerning Robusta in the market is much less than that of Arabica. In this sense, Robusta-growing farmers are much more separated from the consumers in the developed countries.

In this situation, Vietnamese coffee farmers concentrate on producing as much as possible at the cost of quality. And Vietnamese coffee achieved price competitiveness in the world market. In other words, the market mechanism gave the Vietnamese coffee farmers only the strong incentive to produce as much as possible and the farmers responded to this market signal. Fortunately there existed abundant land for coffee growing in the Central Highland. Responding to this market signal, many poor farmers in the densely-populated areas in the Northern and Central Vietnam migrated to the sparsely-populated Central Highland. Vietnamese farmers are clever and also very diligent as is well known, and could achieve a very high level of productivity.[9] If there were no Coffee Crisis such as that occurred in the early 2000s, the Vietnamese coffee industry would have been appraised as a success story of remarkable development. However, what actually happened was to the contrary. Vietnam was often accused of causing the Coffee Crisis by oversupplying coffee to the world market. Because of this oversupply,

[8] The coffee fruit is usually called "coffee cherry" because it looks like a cherry.

[9] See MPI and UNDP (2000a, b, 2001), World Bank et al. (1999), World Bank and DFID (1999) for the general situation of poverty in Vietnam.

they claimed, the world coffee price fell down to a historically-low level of price, though this argument neglects the difference between Arabica and Robusta. The Vietnamese government tried to reduce coffee production not only to help the poor coffee farmers who suffered from the Coffee Crisis but also to respond to this claim. The government recommended to coffee farmers that they shift from growing coffee to other more profitable crops such as pepper. Vietnam could succeed in increasing pepper and other crops. Now Vietnam is the largest pepper exporting country in the world. In spite of these efforts, coffee production did not decrease as expected. To the contrary it still increased except for a few years in the early 2000s.

Another policy was to shift from Robusta to Catimor, a variety of Arabica because Catimor fetches a higher price, though the price of Catimor is lower than other varieties of Arabica. Catimor has the same good characteristics as Robusta such as the leaf disease resistibility and can grow in similar natural conditions as Robusta where Arabica cannot grow. Catimor can be planted at a high density of 5,000–6,000 trees per ha and its productivity can be as high as 3–4 tons per ha. It is sometimes said that it reached as high as 5–6 tons per ha in the experimental field of the Coffee Research Institute in Buon Ma Thuot city, Dak Lak province. After 30 months, it can give the first crop and its productivity can reach up to 2.5 tons per ha in the second crop.

It may seem that a way to solve the problem of oversupply of coffee is to improve the quality of coffee, which will lead to decrease the production volume at the same time as increasing the price. It is inevitable to decrease the production volume if the quality is improved. And more labor input will be needed. This cost will be compensated by the increasing price. However, this policy may not work because the efforts to improve the quality of coffee may not be rewarded. Vietnamese coffee farmers do not seem to be interested in the quality of coffee. They are not interested in what kind of coffee is preferred by the consumers in developing countries. They like to talk how high their productivity. They talk proudly that their productivity is as high as 2–3 tons per hectare, which is much higher than other countries. To the contrary, they do not like to talk about quantity. For example, good quality coffee should be harvested only when the fruits became red, which is called "coffee cherry," but it is much time-consuming and less "efficient." They like to sell as soon as possible when the coffee price is high. They do not care about picking unripe green fruits because the market does not distinguish between ripe and unripe coffee beans. The middlemen buy the coffee beans at the same price irrespective of the quality. This means that there is a very strong incentive to increase their production at the cost of quality and that there is no incentive to improve the quality. The middlemen do not pay enough money for any efforts to improve the quality of coffee. They pay attention to the moisture of coffee beans because it affects the weight and accordingly the amount of money to pay for the farmers. When they buy coffee beans from farmers, they store them in a place, good quality coffee being mixed with low quality one. Thus the price mechanism which encourages farmers to grow high quality coffee does not exist at this stage. Even though Vietnam was often blamed for its overproduction, the Vietnamese farmers are rational in the sense that they are just following the market mechanism. The problem is not on the side of Vietnamese coffee farmers but on the side of the market. So long as the market demands cheap Robusta coffee, Vietnamese farmers will continue to produce cheap coffee beans.

Even though Vietnam may succeed in expanding coffee export as a country, the individual coffee farmers were seriously affected by the Coffee Crisis, especially for the newcomers. In the midst of the coffee bubble in the mid-1990s, many farmers migrated to the Central Highland and began to grow coffee expecting that the high price would continue in the future. But a few years later when they just began to harvest, coffee prices had already decreased and they could not sell at the price as they expected. They could not recover their investment and were left with a large amount of debt. It is difficult to blame the individual farmers as a cause of the Coffee Crisis. They are also the victims of the market mechanism.

If consumers prefer higher quality coffee and are willing to pay higher prices for higher quality as is usually supposed, then our question should be why do the middlemen not pay higher prices for higher quality coffee. One of the reasons is specific to Robusta. Robusta, the main product of Vietnam, targets the low end market such as instant (soluble) coffee. If some undesirable components in the low quality coffee can be removed by recent technological innovation, the manufacturers of soluble coffee may not need high quality coffee even though they may broadcast they are using the "best quality coffee" in the advertisement. As mentioned above, Robusta is not a product for which brand name matters, unlike Arabica. It is no use to put the name of producing countries of Robusta as a country-of-origin on the label of the final products that consumers buy because it will not increase the market value of the products. Even for instant coffee, which may use a lot of Vietnamese coffee, the name of Vietnam may not appear in the label. This is the reason why most of the people do not know the fact that Vietnam is a major coffee exporting country, even though Vietnam is the second largest coffee exporting country in the world.

However, not only the manufacturers but also the consumers in developed countries are responsible for deteriorating quality of coffee and the oversupply in the world coffee market. In the case of instant coffee, consumers usually do not expect high quality but just convenience and cheapness rather than taste. They are much less interested in what condition the coffee they drink is grown in developing countries. Usually consumers cannot even see the green bean, the raw material of instant coffee in their neighborhood, while they sometimes can see the green beans of Arabica at roaster shops. They know much more about Arabica but very little about Robusta. They may have some knowledge about the situation and environment of Arabica-producing countries but not so much about Robusta-producing countries. In this situation, responding to the consumers' knowledge and demand, manufactures of instant coffee may seek cheapness in order to maximize the profit at the cost of farmers and environment. What is worse, they may seek technological innovation to produce good instant coffee with low quality coffee so that they can use cheap low-quality coffee as raw material. This reminds us of the Singer-Prebisch thesis in the classical development economics, which insists that the terms of trade deteriorate for developing countries partly due to technological innovation in developed countries. What is happening in the Robusta market may be just what this thesis insists. Vietnam succeeded in responding to this demand by diligence and achieved very high productivity. However, ironically their success resulted in oversupply and lower price of coffee.

9.4 Solidarity Through Coffee

As mentioned in the previous section, a problem of the market mechanism, which caused the Coffee Crisis, is that the farmers and the consumers are connected to each other only with very limited information such as price. In the case of Robusta, given the price, farmers are interested only in producing as much as possible ignoring the quality while consumers are interested in finding cheap products. Most consumers are not interested in the poverty among the farmers and the environmental destruction, which the coffee that they drink may cause in remote producing countries. Even in the case of Arabica, the situation is almost the same as the case of Robusta. Consumers in developed countries may know the name of the country from which the coffee that they are drinking comes because Arabica coffee is differentiated by the name of producing countries. However, even in this case, they usually don't know the situation of the producing countries. Most of them were not interested in the poverty and environmental destruction, at least before the Coffee Crisis in the early 2000s. It is only after the Coffee Crisis that the difficult situation of coffee farmers in developing countries was broadcast in developed countries by mass media.

When the consumers in developed countries realized the situation of poverty among farmers, they began to know that the affluent society that they are enjoying is built on the poverty of remote countries. Just as we instinctively feel sympathy when we see other people in trouble, we feel sympathy when we hear that other people are struggling in trouble, even though we do not see them directly. Thus our sympathy can be extended globally beyond the national borders and ethnicity. To know the situation is just a starting point to do something to solve the problems.[10]

This was actually what happened and became popular among consumers after the Coffee Crisis. When consumers in developed countries began to know the poverty among coffee farmers, some of them felt sympathy for the poor farmers on the other side of the earth and tried to do something to help them, for example, by paying more for coffee as is the case of fair-trade.[11] This shows that the attitude of consumers can be very different when they know more about the farmers. And this indicates

[10] Sen (1981, 2009) wrote about the case of Bengal Famine. The government underreported the death in the famine, and did not take serious action to save the starving people. What changed the situation was a report of a newspaper on the real situation, by which the government began to take action to save the people in hunger.

[11] It should be mentioned that many of the consumers were enjoying the cheap price. However, this situation is not sustainable because farmers could not continue to grow coffee. Or if they could, they could not maintain the quality because they could not invest at the cheap price. In order to maintain the quality, farmers need to buy more input and to devote more time to take care of coffee trees, which is not profitable at the cheap price.

that the market brings too limited information to the consumers to avoid the problems. The market mechanism does not necessarily bring us to an optimal situation as the economics insists. It is a story in a very limited framework. We need more information to evaluate the situation more fully in order to avoid problems or injustice.[12]

Consumers can go beyond charity and remove injustice in other parts of the earth. For example, if a coffee plantation is using child labor, or if a coffee plantation is destructing environment, consumers can reject the products of the plantation. To the contrary, if we buy its coffee, we are supporting child labor and environmental destruction. When we have the power to avoid the problems but do nothing to do so, we are responsible for the problems. This is called "obligations of power"[13] This is a case that consumers are not responsible for the problems. But consumers may be responsible in some cases. For example, if consumers demand cheap coffee, the farmers may reduce the cost by using child labor, or by not taking care of the environment, and so on. If they cannot reduce the cost, their income will be decreased and they may subside into poverty. In these cases, consumers are partly responsible for the problems, even though it is not clearly defined.[14] Recently consumers began to know these relationships and think about how to avoid them. For this purpose, consumers need to know how the coffee they drink is grown. Now they began to choose coffee not only by the taste but also by the conditions in which it is grown. However, coffee is a global product and therefore it is not easy for consumers in developed countries to see how the farmers in developing countries grow coffee except for special cases. And even if they have the chance to see, they lack the specialist knowledge to judge the situation. Therefore they need neutral intermediary organizations to certify that products are satisfactory in the sense that they do not cause any serious problems. With the certificate on the label of the product, consumers can make sure that the coffee they drink avoids the problems. It may be simply the logos of the organization such as Fair Trade, Rainforest Alliance, UTZ

---

[12] For this purpose, Amartya Sen (1985, 1992, 1997, 1999) proposes the capability approach. The basic idea is that we need more information to evaluate the well-being of people. We cannot measure it only by income because people have different ability to make use of the income. For example, handicapped people or discriminated people can achieve much less than what non-handicapped people or non-discriminated people can do and can be. Instead of income, he proposes to focus on what a person can do and can be, which he calls capability. An application of the capability approach to Vietnam is found in Ikemoto (2001). Injustice can happen when we don't know the situation. We need more information to change our society for the better. Solidarity is a way to increase the information by knowing each other well.

[13] Sen (2009) refers to the obligations of power presented by Gautama Buddha in Sutta Nipata. "Buddha argues there that we have responsibility to animals precisely because of the asymmetry between us, not because of any symmetry that takes us to the need for cooperation. He argues instead that since we are enormously more powerful than the other species, we have some responsibility towards other species that connects exactly with this asymmetry of power." (*The Idea of Justice*, Chap. 9. Plurality of Impartial Reasons, p. 205).

[14] Sen wrote, "As Immanuel Kant argued, many of the obligations that we recognize take the form of what he calls 'imperfect obligations', which are not defined in any particularly precise way, and yet they are neither absent nor negligible" (Sen 2009, Chap. 6. Closed and Open Impartiality, p. 129).

Kapeh (Good Inside), Bird Friendly, and so on. Consumers know from the logo that the products they are consuming are neither violating human rights nor destructing the environment. In this sense, the logo is bringing information on the farmers to the consumers, which the market did not bring, and the consumers may feel solidarity with the farmers by knowing their actual situation.

The relationship is not one-way. The farmers are also affected through the process to earn the certificate. For example, farmers have to learn how to grow coffee in an appropriate way, how to protect the environment, how to take care of the workers, and so on, in order to earn the certificate, though there are many kinds of certificates and the conditions that the certificates require for the farmers may differ among them. They will learn not only the technique to grow coffee but also about human rights and environmental protection which are needed to improve their life. At the same time, they may begin to think about the consumers in remote countries. Coffee farmers are usually separated from consumers and not interested in what kind of coffee consumers prefer, but now they have to think about it. Consumers are not just someone behind the market but human being directly related to each other. By earning the certificate, farmers are connected with consumers and may feel solidarity with the consumers. Now solidarity is established on both sides. If this tie is strengthened, the coffee industry as a global industry will be sustainable.

Unfortunately the proportion of farmers who earn the certificates is still very small but we should not underestimate its impact. For example, a large percentage of consumers know the name of fair trade and a part of them know the meaning of the fair trade, even though only a few percent of them may actually buy the products of fair trade. Similarly on the other hand, the knowledge of the farmers who earned the certificate may spread to the neighboring farmers.

9.5 Further Considerations

- Look for the certified coffee sold around you. Where are the coffee beans grown? What does the certificate mean to, for example, poverty eradication, environmental protection, human rights, or any other?
- Look for certified products similar to the case of coffee. What does the certificate mean?

References

Gresser C, Tickell S (2002) Mugged: poverty in your coffee cup. Oxfam international research paper

Ikemoto Y (2001) Poverty, ethnic minority, and culture: a case in Vietnam. In: Presented at the conference on justice and poverty: examining Sen's capability approach, 5–7 June 2001, Von Hügel Institute, St Edmund's College, University of Cambridge

Ikemoto Y, H'wen NK (2003) Coffee. In: JICA and MPI (eds) Growing sub-sectors in Vietnamese agriculture

MPI (Ministry of Planning and Investment, Vietnam) and UNDP (2000a) A rural social development and poverty reduction strategy for Viet Nam
MPI and UNDP (2000b) Draft report on agriculture and rural development in Viet Nam
MPI and UNDP (2001) A rural social development and poverty reduction strategy for Viet Nam
Phan T, H'wen NK, Ikemoto Y (eds) (2007) Coffee in Vietnam's central highlands: historical, anthropological and economic perspectives. Vietnam National University Hochiminh City Press, Ho Chi Minh City, Vietnam
Sen A (1981) Poverty and famines: an essay on entitlement and deprivation. Oxford University Press, Oxford
Sen A (1985) Commodities and capabilities. North-Holland, Amsterdam
Sen A (1992) Inequality reexamined. Oxford University Press, Oxford
Sen A (1997) On economic inequality. In: Foster J, Sen A (eds) On economic inequality after a quarterly century. Clarendon Press, Oxford
Sen A (1999) Development as freedom. Oxford University Press, Oxford
Sen A (2009) The idea of justice. Allen Lane & Harvard University Press, London
UN Conference on Trade and Development (UNCTD) and CyclOple (2000) World commodity survey; 2000–2001
World Bank (2001) World development report 2000/2001: attacking poverty. Oxford University Press, New York
World Bank and DFID (1999) Vietnam: voices of the poor. The World Bank, Vietnam
World Bank et al (1999) Vietnam development report 2000, attacking poverty, Hanoi

Chapter 10
Development of Social Business in Korea

Ki-Hueng Kim

Abstract In Korea, the participation of social enterprises is actively practiced through enacting the Social Enterprise Promotion Act of 2007. To be a social enterprise, an organization must be certified by the Minister of Employment and Labor according to the Social Enterprise Promotion Act. The Korean government promoted making the Social Enterprise Promotion Ordinances appropriate to each locality by each local government based on the Social Enterprise Promotion Act. Heuksalim is promoting several social activities such as the urban agriculture project to strengthen the solidarity with urban consumers and traditional seed preservation as a local resource.

Keywords Social Enterprise Promotion Act · Government support · Certification of social enterprise · Preliminary social enterprise

10.1 Introduction

Development of social enterprises in Korea began with social civic groups in the 1990s. Active supports by government stimulated promotion of social enterprises by enacting the Social Enterprise Promotion Act in 2007. After this, social enterprises have been pushed ahead based on the certification system which is the source of several other types of support by the government.

Additionally, since 2010 local governments have proposed Ordinances and Regulations to grow the "preliminary social enterprises" through participation of various kinds of groups that pursue social purposes. However, it has been pointed out that these Ordinances and Regulations by the local governments have almost uniform contents throughout the country rather than reflecting the unique local conditions and characteristics.

K.-H. Kim (✉)
Chungnam Development Institute, 73-26 Yeonsuwon-gil, Gongju-si,
Chungcheongnam-do, South Korea
e-mail: kihuengkim@gmail.com

N. Matsui and Y. Ikemoto (eds.), *Solidarity Economy and Social Business*,
SpringerBriefs in Economics, DOI 10.1007/978-4-431-55471-4_10

In fact, social enterprises in Korea emphasize too much on the job creation and providing services in order to get certification rather than being concerned about the fundamental discernment about the meaning of "social." This indicates that the concept of social enterprise may not be clear to those who participate in certification processes even though definition exists by law. Moreover, the role and perspective of social enterprises still have ambiguity in Korea. Meanwhile, recently it is true that the recognition of social enterprise from a lot of civic groups is expanding. Furthermore it is difficult to deny that there are many social enterprises which are focusing on social concern rather than on profit.

In this chapter, the current situation and the development of social enterprises promoted and based on the Social Enterprise Promotion Act are examined. A case study of certified social enterprise is shown in Sect. 10.4.

10.2 Social Enterprise Promotion Act

Social enterprises in Korea began as a way to solve the problem of unemployment among vulnerable social groups and to expand the provision of social services. In the Social Enterprise Promotion Act, "social services" refers to services in education, health, social welfare, environment and culture and other services appropriate to this law, whose area is prescribed by Presidential Decree.

The participation of enterprises has actively been promoted through enacting the Social Enterprise Promotion Act since 2007. In this Act, "social enterprise" is defined as an organization which is engaged in the business activities of producing and selling goods and services while pursuing the social purpose of enhancing the quality of lives of local residents by means of providing social services and creating jobs for the disadvantaged (Article 2). In this Act, "the disadvantaged" means people who have difficulty in purchasing social services necessary for themselves at a market price, the detailed criteria thereof shall be determined by Presidential Decree.

The purpose of this Act is to contribute to the integration of society as well as to the enhancement of the quality of the people's lives thereof, by means of expanding social services, which are not sufficiently provided in society, and creating jobs (Article 1). This Act was amended twice in 2010 and 2012. Table 10.1 shows the development of social enterprises in Korea.

Social enterprise began with civic community movements such as Workers' Production Cooperatives, etc. in poor regions in the early 1990s. The Korean government started a rehabilitation and self-support project for the handicapped. In 1996 the Self-support project targeted to the poor was implemented by the Ministry of Welfare. In 1997 the Public Working program was launched at the time of the economic crisis. In 1999 the National Basic Living Security Act was enacted to help the self-support of the poorest class. In 2003 the Social Job Creation and Social Service project began for the people who are being under the poverty threshold and vulnerable. Finally in the 2007 Social Enterprise Promotion Act was enacted, and 36 enterprises were certified initially.

Table 10.1 Development of social enterprises in Korea

Date	Contents
Early 1990s	Production community movement
Late 1990s	Self-support project by government
1997	Economic crisis
1999	National Basic Living Security Act enacted
2003	Social job project-social service started
Jan. 2007	Social Enterprise Promotion Act enacted
2008	Five years plan for social enterprise promotion
Jun. 2010	Social Enterprise Promotion Act amended
Dec. 2010	Korea Social Enterprise Promotion Agency established (http://socialenterprise.or.kr)
Feb. 2012	Social Enterprise Promotion Act amended

Source Work Together Foundation (2012)

Table 10.2 Types of social enterprises by main purpose

Types	Contents
Job-creation type	To offer jobs to vulnerable social groups
Social service provision type	To provide social services to vulnerable social groups
Local community contribution type	To contribute to the local community
Mixed type	To offer jobs to vulnerable social groups and at the same time to provide social services to vulnerable social groups
Other types	Though the main purpose is to provide social services, it is hard to judge the realization of social purposes with the ratio of the employment of vulnerable social groups or the ratio of the provision of social services as the organization is doing businesses for many random people

Source Korea Social Enterprise Promotion Agency (http://socialenterprise.or.kr)

To be a social enterprise, an organization must be certified by the Minister of Employment and Labor according to the Social Enterprise Promotion Act. As of June 2013, a total of 828 companies were certified as social enterprises. To be certified as a social enterprise, an organization must first have an independent organizational type to be certified as a social enterprise (Social Enterprise Promotion Act, Article 8) as follows: a corporation or cooperative according to Civil Act or a company according to the Commercial Act, a public corporation according to the Establishment and Operation of Public Corporations Act, a nonprofit civic organization according to the Support for Non-profit Civic Organizations Act, a social welfare corporation according to the Social Welfare Projects Act, a living cooperative according to the Consumer Living Cooperative Act, and other non-profit organizations according to other laws. These organizations must belong to one of the five types of organization according to the main purpose (Table 10.2).

Table 10.3 Evaluating social purposes by types

Types	Contents
Job-creation type	The ratio of employment of vulnerable social groups is more than 30 %
Social service provision type	The ratio of the vulnerable social groups receiving social services is more than 30 %
Local community contribution type	The ratio of the population of vulnerable social groups residing in the region of the location of the relevant organization, or the ratio of the vulnerable social groups receiving social services is more than 20 %
Mixed type	The ratio of employment of vulnerable social groups and the ratio of the vulnerable social groups receiving social services is more than 20 % respectively
Other types	If it is hard to judge the realization of social purposes, it is determined by the social enterprise committee

Source Korea Social Enterprise Promotion Agency (http://socialenterprise.or.kr)

Table 10.3 shows the evaluation of social purposes such as the provision of jobs for vulnerable social groups or social services by each type. The performance of the realization of social purpose is evaluated for the following 6 months for the same time period of income through business activities.

The total income through business activities should be more than 30 % of the total labor cost for the past 6 months to qualify for the application. Government subsidies and other donations are not included in this income. However, the income through public sales such as provision of goods and services, and participating in voucher projects, etc. are included in this total income. The total labor cost indicates the total amount actually paid to the workers regardless of the government subsidy for labor cost. Additionally according to the reinvestment of profits, when distributable profits remain during a fiscal year, more than two thirds of the profits shall be reinvested for social purposes. The details of reinvestment will be comprehensively evaluated for certification.

In Korea, there is a category of "preliminary" social enterprise. That is, when an organization satisfies the minimum legal conditions to be certified as a social enterprise, but does not meet some requirements such as profit structure, the ministers of the central government and local government may designate it as a preliminary social enterprise to be certified in the near future as a social enterprise.

There are two types of preliminary social enterprises, the regional type and the divisional type. The former one was introduced to promote the social enterprises suited to regional characteristics by the National Employment Strategy Meeting in August 2010. The purpose is to make local governments participate in stabilizing local employment and in creating jobs more actively. The latter type is introduced for the government ministry to certify as the social enterprise to promote diversified local development work since 2013.

Duration is for 1 year after the issuance of the designation certificate, and may be extended annually through reexamination for a maximum of 3 years. In

Table 10.4 Differences between social enterprises and preliminary social enterprises

Classification	Social enterprise	Preliminary social enterprise
Law	Social Enterprise Promotion Act	Ordinance and regulations on the support for the promotion of social enterprises
Requirements for certification	Type of organization	Type of organization
	Conduct business activities by hiring paid workers	Conduct business activities by hiring paid workers (regardless of sales volume)
	Realize social purposes	Realize social purposes
	Decisions are made with the participation of stakeholders	Reinvest more than two thirds of the profits for the realization of social purposes
	Make profits through business activities	
	Must have articles of association and regulations	
	Reinvest more than two thirds of the profits for the realization of social purposes	

Source Korea Social Enterprise Promotion Agency (http://socialenterprise.or.kr)

2013, all sixteen local governments are promoting preliminary social enterprises. The differences between social enterprises and preliminary social enterprises are shown in Table 10.4.

When social enterprises are certified, the Korean government by law gives support to those social enterprises in the following four items;

(1) The Minister of Labor may provide various support such as specialized advice, information, etc. in areas of administration, technology, tax, labor, accounting, etc. which is needed for the operation of a social enterprise. (Article 10: Operation Support)
(2) The nation or a local government may support or finance site expenses, facility expenses, etc. or lease state-owned land and co-owned land, which is necessary for the establishment or operation of a social enterprise. (Article 11: Support for Facility Expenses)
(3) The nation and a local government may reduce national tax and local tax as determined by the Corporate Tax Act, the Restriction of Special Taxation Act, and the Local Tax Act. The nation may support a part of employment insurance premium and industrial accident compensation insurance premium. (Article 13: Tax Reduction and Support for Social Insurance Premium)
(4) The Minister of Labor may provide a social enterprise providing social service with financial support such as labor costs, operating expenses, consultation expenses, etc. within the limit of the budget through public recruitment and examination. (Article 14: Financial Assistance for a Social Enterprise Providing Social Service)

Table 10.5 Support programs to social enterprises

	Support program	Target
Direct support	Create social jobs	Social enterprise
		Preliminary social enterprises
	Professional consulting	Social enterprise
Indirect support	Costs for business development	Social enterprise
		Preliminary social enterprises
	Management consulting	Social enterprise
		Preliminary social enterprises
	Tax reduction	Social enterprise
	Premium of four major insurances	Social enterprise
	Giving loans	Social enterprise
		Preliminary social enterprises
	Preferential purchase by public institutions	Social enterprise
Environmental support	Academy and education	Social enterprise
		Preliminary social enterprises
	Social venture contest	Youth or anybody
	Fostering youths to be social entrepreneurs	Those who want to do a business (19–39 years 50 %)
	Pro bono	Social enterprise
		Preliminary social enterprises
	Network	Social enterprise
		Preliminary social enterprises

Source Korea Social Enterprise Promotion Agency (http://socialenterprise.or.kr)

These supports are divided into three categories as direct support, indirect support and environmental support (see Table 10.5). Direct support is most helpful to an organization performing as the social business. Creating social jobs programs includes support for personnel expenses and for professional consulting. Personnel expenses include the labor cost of the participants when a social enterprise joins the job-creating social programs. Additionally minimum wage and premiums of four major insurances are supported up to 9 % of the personnel expenses. When this is adopted, the differential rates of support fund are applied for each year. As to social enterprise, 90 % of the personnel expenses are paid for by the government the first year, 80 % for the second year, and 70 % for the third year. In the case of "preliminary" social enterprise, in the first year 100 % is paid for and 90 % in the second year. Social enterprise support is offered for a maximum of up to 3 years and up to 2 years for preliminary social enterprise. As to professional consulting, support as a part of expenses for management, accounting and marketing, a social enterprise may be supported a maximum of 2 million won per month and three persons for 3 years. The differential rates of self-bearing expenses are adopted for each year, that is, the first year is 20 %, the second year 30 % and the third year 50 %.

Table 10.6 shows the results of social enterprise promotion for the last 3 years from 2007 to 2010 by those supports from the government. According

Table 10.6 Results of social enterprise, 2007–2010

	2007	2010
Total organization certified	51	501
Total workers employed	2,539	13,443
Disadvantaged workers employed	1,403	8,227
Ratio to labor force population	0.0104 %	0.0543 %
Total social service beneficiary	26,121	6,562,077
Total disadvantaged beneficiary	17,166	3,890,202
Total sales	46.4 billion won	376.5 billion won
Total net profit during the term	4.6 billion won	7.1 billion won
Total non-operating profit	21.3 billion won	108.4 billion won

Source Work Together Foundation (2012)

to the Ministry of Employment and Labor (2012), the total number of certified organizations has increased by 450 from 2007 to 2010. The total number of social service beneficiaries has increased to 251 times as much for 3 years and the total number of disadvantaged beneficiary has increased to 227 times at the same time. Total sales have increased to 8.1 times and total net profit during the term has increased to 1.54 times. Total sales per worker employed were 28 million won in 2010, while that of 2007 were 18 million won. Meanwhile, government support policies are effective compared to other job programs. It is calculated that the ratio of subsidy to sales was 279.9 % (2009). There has been stable growth in spite of some regional and sectoral differences. However profitability was very low in that net profit rate to total sales was 1.8 %. This occurred from inefficient cost structure due to the high sales cost and labor cost, difficulty in pricing near to the market price, and inadequate sales force due to the lack of professional labor force. Additional hiring of employees for the purpose of reinvestment for social purpose includes 22 persons and hiring additional disadvantaged employees includes 23 persons (2009). Internally accumulated money is the biggest part for reinvestment of profit. Other items for reinvestment are directed towards the benefit of members, and contribution to local society among others.

10.3 Local Government Efforts: Chungcheongbuk-do Case

The Korean government encouraged each local government to make Social Enterprise Promotion Ordinances to be appropriate to their own localities based on the Social Enterprise Promotion Act. By examining them, however, it became clear that the stipulations of the ordinance and regulations by many local governments were quite similar. Jang et al. (2010) pointed out that the ordinances do not specify the concrete objectives in order to revitalize the social enterprises, even though ordinances are necessary to provide the evidences to secure the funds.

Table 10.7 Current situation of social enterprises in Chungcheongbuk-do

	Details	Number of social enterprises
Business sector (64)	Education	2
	Culture and art	2
	Environment	6
	Local food	8
	Cleaning and disinfection	12
	Manufacturing	15
	Services	19
Paid workers (49)	Less than 6 workers	10
	6-20	25
	21–50	9
	51–100	4
	More than 101 workers	1
Organization form (64)	A living cooperative	1
	Agricultural association	4
	Social welfare corporation	4
	A corporation	5
	Non-profit organizations	10
	A company	40
Achieving social purposes (49)	Job-creation type	28
	Social service provision type	4
	Mixed type	10
	Local community contribution type	0
	Other types	7

Source Chungcheongbuk-do (2012)

Table 10.7 shows a case of the concrete actions of social enterprises in local government of Chungcheongbuk-do (Shortly, Chungbuk).

In 2012 there were 26 social enterprises and 34 preliminary social enterprises in total 60 certified social enterprises in Chungbuk. Chungbuk preliminary social enterprises have been increasing every year since 2010. Table 10.7 shows the current conditions of social enterprises in Chungbuk. In the business sector, the services category is the biggest class. And these days the local food sector is growing gradually. This means that some organizations using local agricultural productions have been promoting local-based economy with the solidarity between farmers and citizens and this gives the expansion of local activities and good reputation to the community. As for paid workers 6–20 are the biggest class with 25 workers and less than 6 are the next with 10 workers. As for organization form, companies according to the Commercial Act compose the biggest number category with 40 and non-profit organizations (NPO) are the next biggest with 10.

Park (2012) pointed out that the remarkable increase of social enterprises occurred through the transformation from the government support program such as the Self-support Project by the Ministry of Welfare, the Local Public Job Program by the Ministry of Security and Public Administration and so on to the certification of social enterprises, and the participation of private corporations to the preliminary social enterprises, which is relatively easy.

10.4 A Case Study: Heuksalim

In this section, the case of organic agricultural group certified as social enterprise in Chungbuk, Heuksalim is examined. Initially, it was started by the local farmers for research on organic agriculture as the Guesan Study Group of Microorganism in Guesan of Chungbuk. Later this group has been promoting the organic agricultural technique and development, supports, education for farmers, and certification work.

In 1996, Heuksalim Institute was established as a corporation and in 1999 it changed to the incorporated Heuksalim as the result of expansion of its environment-friendly agricultural materials work. In 2002 it was certified as the first certification body for environment-friendly agriculture in responding to the request of local farmers. It should be pointed out that the certification system in Korea is not only to certify environment-friendly agricultural products but also to promote comprehensive environment-friendly agriculture including education and promotion activities for farmers. This shows the unique characteristics of the development of organic agriculture in Korea, see also Sect. 8.3 of this book, in between 2011 and (Kim 2011). The certification process was executed by an independent body having neutral stance. Meanwhile, this work was transferred to a new institute, Korea Institute for Agricultural Products and Food Certification, to assure strictly the third-party position of certification since 2009 and was completely separated from Heuksalim in June 2013.

The Heuksalim Institute continued to implement farmers' education, publication of newspapers keeping the movement's characteristics such as the traditional agriculture committee which is performing the gathering and preserving of traditional seeds based on field research for farmers. They have gathered 600 varieties of traditional seeds since 2010. They made an illustrated guide to traditional crops resources with the support of local governments to preserve the agricultural regional resources which are at risk for becoming extinct. This kind of activity contributes to local communities by way of utilization of local resources with local farmers. That is called "social purpose." Table 10.8 shows the organization of Heuksalim.

Heuksalim has been certified as the social enterprise since 2008 when the Social Enterprise Promotion Act was enacted a year later. Even though those activities of Heuksalim Institute itself involved social purpose, it was necessary to make a new corporation for organic agricultural project groups to get certified as social enterprises. The main work is preserving traditional seeds. At first they applied for job-creation type as a social enterprise and they got minimum wage of 850 thousand won per one person. Farmers are included as a vulnerable group

Table 10.8 Organization of Heuksalim

	Heuksalim Institute	Heuksalim (Inc.)	Agricultural corporation Heuksalim	Korea agricultural products and food certification
Start	1996	1999	2007	2009
Employee	5	15	45	5
Work	Farmers' education, publication of newspaper and preservation of traditional seeds	Production and sales of environment-friendly agricultural materials	Wholesale, delivery and store	Certification

so that 20 farmers out of 60 paid workers were also supported by the government. Actually these farmers had been distributing their agricultural products to Heuksalim, thus they are just doing organic farming using the traditional seeds as usual. Additional works include packing products, management of production and working at organic product stores.

The traditional seed project was appropriate for a social purpose, and the intention of which was to contribute to development and preservation of the traditional local agriculture. Nevertheless, it is just beginning to run and the profit from it is not so high. As a result, this project for social enterprise was finished 3 years later since it was not sustainable in job creation. Later, Heuksalim considered that running business with social purpose has a limit and risk. Originally they had social activities such as disseminating the values of organic agriculture and promoting the preservation of traditional seed. But, it was found difficult to make good relationships with consumers by supplying organic agricultural products.

In 2007, Heuksalim Food as an agricultural corporation was established to promote the marketing business of agricultural products. They were certified as a preliminary social enterprise in November 2010, then became a social enterprise 3 years later. Heuksalim Food was separated into three projects, store sales, internet sales promotion, and whole sales. Its main work since April 2009 has been internet sales promotion of a delivery service for a vegetable box scheme (called Kuromi here). In March 2013 there were one thousand consumers and 200 total producers among which the core producers were 80.

Those farmers who originally had contracts with Hansalim and iCoop (Both are a Consumer Cooperative), distributed their remaining products after sales to Hansalim and iCoop since Heuksalim Food's order was small and was just beginning to get farmers involved. Kuromi is delivered every Thursday. Consumers put in their orders by Thursday of the previous week, then producers arrange products by next Tuesday. They are ready to be delivered on Wednesday. Delivery service is carried out by the post office and this cost is included in the price of Kuromi. As to individual store businesses, currently there are six places and three of them are managed directly by Heuksalim Food. Here they get orders every day. Delivery to stores is done by using their own trucks because there is not so much quantity. Lastly, according to wholesale business, they supply their products, mainly vegetables, to e-Mart (a Korean large retailer). These vegetables are cultivated by farmers near the Heuksalim distribution center. Rice and eggs are brought from the same province and fruits are from all over the country. Currently, the wholesale consists of 70 % out of total sales. Kuromi consists of 20 % and store business 10 %. However, the share of the wholesale business is hoped to be reduced to 50 % and Kuromi business is expected to grow higher in near future.

Support for the labor cost will be continued for 3 years. For a minimum wage of 1.05 million won, 90 % of it will be paid for the first year, 70 % for the second year and 50 % for the third year. Fifteen vulnerable persons have been supported in this regard since 2013. The main work of the Kuromi project is not only to provide job creation but also to supply the social services of providing organic agricultural products free of charge to those who are identified as vulnerable groups. Additionally they supply organic products to their employees at a half price.

Meanwhile, Heuksalim cooperates with urban agriculture businesses. One of them is urban agriculture project in Nodle Island and another is the Gwanghwamun park area in Seoul. The former is the cropping experience program by consumers who are members of the consumers association in Han River in Seoul. Participants who want to do farming will have to pay for the rest of 0.1 million won per 3.3 square meters to cultivate their own crops in the field for a year. The latter is the rice farming project to plant and cultivate rice instead of flowers in a square of central Seoul. This was introduced by an artists group and farmers in Seoul. Heuksalm's activities include supporting agricultural techniques such as supply seed and agricultural training here. These group members are planting the traditional seeds of rice and cereals. Furthermore, Heuksalim initiated a rooftop garden project at the library in Gwangjin district in Seoul. For this kind of activity, Heuksalim (Inc.) is selling agricultural materials needed for urban agriculture and the Heuksalim Institute gives support for the management part, for example, technical training.

These days, Heuksalim is operating the training programs. One of them is the "long term return to farming school" by organizing seminars and agricultural fieldwork in Heuksalim farm from April to November. Currently there are four teaching staff members and five students. Another area of activity is an overseas program, which is sending staff to the Republic of Mozambique and Democratic Republic of the Congo in Africa to help support their agricultural training for 6 months. And one more staff is dispatched to Research Institute of Organic Agriculture (FiBL) in Switzerland.

Heuksalim has been promoting several social activities such as the urban agriculture project to strengthen the solidarity with urban consumers. This shows the importance of factors that the social enterprises ideally should have. It indicates a possibility of a synergy in social enterprise's activities through different activities. Through the organic agricultural products, social enterprise can not only have the relationship between production and sales but also create sustainable relationships based on mutual understanding. This kind of relationship and understanding can make an opportunity to connect people between urban and rural areas by way of participating in the activities of urban agriculture. The traditional seeds in this urban farm project can contribute to utilization and preservation of the local resources. This kind of solidarity broadens the business chance to provide the local services to the broader community and to promote sustainable job creation.

10.5 Further Considerations

- Consider how to continue to be a sustainable organization as a social enterprise after support from government ends.
- Think over the social roles of the social enterprise other than the certification.

References

Jang W-J, Park D-H, Yoo K-H (2010) A study on local government support system to social enterprise: focusing on social enterprise promotion ordinances. Korean Local Gov Law Assoc 26(10):2 (In Korean)

Kim K-H (2011) Local based organic agriculture: experience of Japan and Korea. Tsukuba-shobo, Japan (In Japanese)

Park D-H (2012) Current condition and issue of social enterprise in Chungbuk. Chungcheongbuk-do Business Fair Data, Chungcheongbuk-do (In Korean)

Work Together Foundation (2012) Social enterprise guide book: hope future, the way together. The Ministry of Employment and Labor, Korea (In Korean). The Ministry of Employment and Labor. Social Enterprise Promotion Act

Index

N. Matsui and Y. Ikemoto (eds.), *Solidarity Economy and Social Business*,
SpringerBriefs in Economics, DOI 10.1007/978-4-431-55471-4

MIX
Papier aus verantwortungsvollen Quellen
Paper from responsible sources
FSC® C105338

If you have any concerns about our products,
you can contact us on
ProductSafety@springernature.com

In case Publisher is established outside the EU,
the EU authorized representative is:
Springer Nature Customer Service Center GmbH
Europaplatz 3, 69115 Heidelberg, Germany

Printed by Libri Plureos GmbH
in Hamburg, Germany